CONTENT AREA READING
TEACHERS, TEXTS, STUDENTS

Timothy C. Standal

Ruth E. Betza

PRENTICE HALL, Englewood Cliffs, New Jersey 07632

Library of Congress Cataloging-in-Publication Data

Standal, Timothy C.,
   Content area reading.

   Bibliography: p.
   Includes index.
   1. Content area reading. I. Betza, Ruth E.,
1948-   . II. Title.
LB1050.455.S73 1989   428.4'07   88-32294
ISBN 0-13-171356-6

Editorial/production supervision and
  interior design: Lynda Griffiths
Manufacturing buyer: Peter Havens

Printed in the United States of America

10 9 8 7 6 5 4 3 2 1

ISBN   0-13-171356-6

PRENTICE-HALL INTERNATIONAL (UK) LIMITED, *London*
PRENTICE-HALL OF AUSTRALIA PTY. LIMITED, *Sydney*
PRENTICE-HALL CANADA INC. *Toronto*
PRENTICE-HALL HISPANOAMERICANA, S.A., *Mexico*
PRENTICE-HALL OF INDIA PRIVATE LIMITED, *New Delhi*
PRENTICE-HALL OF JAPAN, INC., *Tokyo*
SIMON & SCHUSTER ASIA PTE. LTD., *Singapore*
EDITORA PRENTICE-HALL DO BRASIL, LTDA., *Rio de Janeiro*

To my children, Katherine, Elizabeth, Peter, and Gregory,
and to my wife, JL.
They believe, as I do, the words of Groucho Marx:
"Outside of a dog, books are man's best friend.
Inside of a dog, it's too dark to read."

T.C.S

To my husband, Hans Grage,
and to the students who will enjoy this book.

R.E.B.

CONTENTS

PREFACE

The goal of this book is not to make you a reading teacher. Rather, the goal is to help make you a better teacher of whatever content area you represent. Thus, we wrote *Content Area Reading: Teachers, Texts, Students* for the content teacher who is interested in reading techniques that she or he can use, not for the reading specialist with an interest in content area reading. The working assumptions are that the book will be used in a first or second course in content area reading and that the course is for content teachers.

In order to begin to do that, the first chapter is devoted to a discussion of the reading process and the factors that influence that process. The chapter concludes with an explanation of how those factors relate to the various chapters in the book. We regard that chapter as the one most central to the book and hope you will study it carefully.

Throughout this book we have tried to present essential information in a clear and readable way and have tried to balance the "why" of things with examples of the "what." Rather than offer a cookbook of every possible recipe for reading in a content area classroom, we have limited the discussions to the ideas that we have found most useful and that we feel are most relevant for you.

ACKNOWLEDGMENTS

We wish to express our appreciation to all the students in Tim's content area reading classes at the University of Washington who read this book, commented on it, made useful suggestions, and offered encouragement.

These teachers, both in-service and pre-service, were endlessly patient with the earliest versions, typos and all, and wonderfully encouraging in their responses to the later versions of this text. Thank you.

I (TCS) want to express my respect and gratitude to a dozen years' worth of content area teachers in my courses, seminars, and workshops who taught me so much about their various disciplines. Mine was often the only reading course they had ever taken or ever would take and that fact helped to keep me focused on what is sensible and practical.

Thanks are due also to Virginia Stimpson of Mercer Island High School for sharing her experiences with and her guidelines for the use of journals in mathematics, physics, and computer programming, and to Chris Fuller for reading and commenting on the chapters on writing.

The line drawings that introduce each chapter and all the photographs are by Jerry Purcell of the University of Washington, College of Education staff. Thanks, Jerry. All photographs were taken at Eastside Catholic High School in Bellevue, Washington. Thanks to faculty, students, and staff.

Special thanks to Lynn Caddey Schweber, sharp-eyed proofreader and creator of the index.

Finally, the assistance of our editor, Carol Wada, at Prentice Hall, was invaluable.

Many helped, of course. Kudos to them. And, naturally, brickbats, if any, should be aimed at us.

CONTENT AREA READING

TEACHERS, TEXTS, STUDENTS

EARLY WRITING

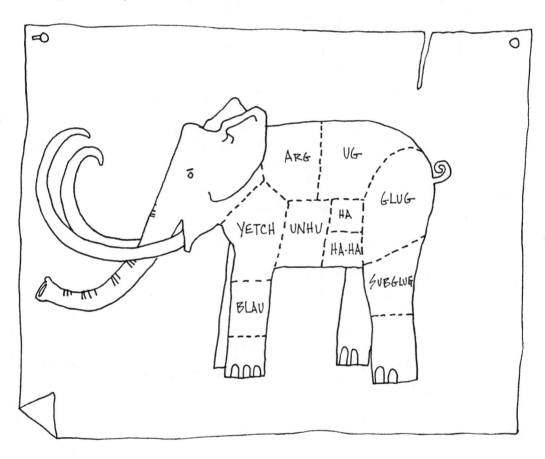

1

READING AND THE CONTENT AREAS

You are a reader. If you weren't, you wouldn't have gotten this far. As a reader you have mastered, at least to some degree, what has been characterized as the second most impressive intellectual feat of which humans are capable. (The first is learning to talk.) Still, as a skilled reader, you probably pay scant attention to your impressive ability. You accept it. It is a powerful skill of incredible, almost limitless utility—and you've got it.

Modern society does not simply demand the skill of reading, it assumes it. Society assumes every one of its postelementary school members is a competent processor of print. It is impossible, without great care and planning, to go through twenty-four hours without reading something. We challenge you to try it. If you accept our challenge, here are some pointers. Don't drive anywhere. There are road signs everywhere and, besides, your car is filled with print. Don't plan to hide in a bookless room and watch television. There is a great deal of print on TV, both in the foreground in the form of advertisements and in the background in the form of signs of one sort and another. Staying in the wilderness for twenty-four hours might work if you remove all the labels from your clothing and camping gear first. You might also have someone go ahead of you as you make your way to your camping spot to remove all print in the form of food wrappers and drink containers scattered along the trail. Your best bet is to use a blindfold.

The point is that the skill of reading is unavoidable in modern life, perhaps more so than most of us realize. But more important than that, reading is crucial to your work as a teacher. Your ability to read accounts for a great part of your own learning, and the reading you assign should account for a great part of your students' learning.

Reading is a process subject. We do not teach people to read so that they can enrich their lives through the adventures of Dick and Jane (or any other basal reader character). We teach them to read so that they can use the skill in a myriad of ways from enlightenment to escape, from exploration to baking the best chocolate chip cookies possible. Mathematics, at least at its lower levels, is also a process subject. We do not teach people to add, subtract, multiply, and divide so that they can spend their lives determining how many apples Farmer Brown sold in October and whether she made any money at it. We teach those things because they are important and useful skills to have for a host of reasons.

Content subjects such as the various sciences and social studies are, on the other hand, studied through reading and lecture and other ways for the information to be gained. Of course, there is a process to these content areas and that process is important. But the focus is on the content. By giving you a background in reading and some ideas and techniques to better use reading, we hope to help you convey to your students the content and process of whatever discipline you represent.

Although the goal of this book is not to turn you into a reading teacher but is, instead, to offer you information and techniques that will help make you a better teacher of whatever you teach, the better you understand the skill, the better you will be able to use it. For this reason, we next present a definition of reading that we refer to throughout this book.

READING: A DEFINITION

Defining the pieces of a skill is not the same thing as defining the skill itself. For example, we are sure that it is possible to measure and describe the components of an excellent tennis serve. But we are equally sure that a definition by bits and pieces is not a definition or description of an expert's serve. The same may be said of the discussion of the bits and pieces of reading that follows. We hope that the discussion is instructive, however, we concede that it is not a complete description.

Decoding

When a person reads something, as you are reading this, there is measurable physiological engagement. The eyes move from point to point along the line of print. The resting places are called *fixations* and the movements are called *saccades*. There is also measurable neuro-electrical activity. Those things, and others that need not be detailed in this book, account for what we shall refer to as the **physiological** component of reading.

Along with physiological engagement, reading involves some **phonological** engagement as well. The muscles of articulation move in ways similar to or approximating the muscular movements of speech. This suggests that when you read, to paraphrase Shakespeare, you speak to your mind's ear. Although phonological engagement may not occur all of the time, it occurs often enough to suggest that it is the normal condition of reading. If you have ever had the opportunity to observe novice readers reading "silently," you know that the reading is anything but silent. Though the audible subvocalization exhibited by beginning readers eventually disappears, subvocalization—speaking to the mind's ear—apparently never does.

Thus far, we have a physiological and a phonological component. Think of these as the mechanisms of "seeing it" and "saying it" respectively. You will notice that we have said nothing up to this point about understanding. Seeing it and saying it may be thought of as **decoding,** which is a necessary but not sufficient prerequisite to understanding. Consider the word *cordelle*. Its proper pronunciation is not tricky. You can see it and say it, but chances are you don't know what it means. You can decode it but not understand it.

As a secondary or upper elementary content teacher, you are not expected to teach the skills of decoding. You may find that in teaching vocabulary to your students you will occasionally have to help them learn the pronunciation of new words but, beyond that, the decoding process should be firmly in place for most students. Even though we realize that some of you will have students who have reading difficulties in the physiological and phonological realms — that is, students who are nondecoders — these issues are out of the scope of this book.

In this book, our interest lies in ways you as a content area teacher can easily improve your students' reading comprehension. The following discussion of **understanding,** with its subheadings of semantics, syntax, and experience, forms the basis for our views of reading in the rest of the book. In it, we find the source of much of the reading information that can help you better teach your content area. Let us consider them one at a time.

Understanding

Understanding an utterance, in speech or in print, depends on word knowledge (semantic knowledge), the ordering in which the word appears (syntax), and experience. Semantic and syntactic knowledge are subsets of experience, but for our purposes in this discussion we will treat them separately.

Semantic ability, or vocabulary, includes not only word meaning but shades of meaning, literal as well as figurative. Because words can have different forms and different meanings, it is hard to measure vocabulary size and its influence on reading ability. Nonetheless, important studies and collections (Davis, 1944, 1968; Anderson and Freebody, 1981; McKeown and Curtis, 1987) have identified vocabulary as the single most important factor in reading comprehension. It seems safe to say that the degree to which vocabulary is deficient is an indication of the degree to which understanding of a text will also be deficient.

Syntax means that we understand and expect sentence constructions such as:

The geese squawked when they were thrown the zucchini from the garden.

Some other word orders are simply impermissible in the English language, as in:

Thrown squawked zucchini the were they when geese garden the the from.

Knowledge of syntax, allowable word order, is almost a given. There is evidence to suggest that for native speakers the syntactic system of English is for all reasonable purposes fully in place by age ten (Chomsky, 1969). Occasionally, in reading an old book, for example, we may be jarred a bit by the style of sentence construction. But even that is relatively short-lived. We usually get used to it amazingly quickly. Sometimes the syntax in a textbook is so convoluted that readers have difficulty. In Chapter 3, we suggest a way to anticipate this problem. However, for present purposes, we will regard syntactic ability for native speakers as a given.

Experience accounts for an incredibly potent piece of the understanding we may gain from reading. It is becoming increasingly obvious that the more experience we have to bring to bear on what we read, the more we can get out of it. The more we know, the more we can know (see, for example, Anderson and Pearson, 1984). Thus, you may find that reading something about your own discipline is relatively easy and be surprised to find that someone without your background has trouble with it. In addition, what we know directs what we notice and remember. For example, in one study (Spilich, Vesonder, Chiesi, and Voss, 1979), people who knew a lot about baseball remembered details such as the plays after listening to a taped passage about baseball. In contrast, people who knew little about baseball recalled details such as the color of the umpire's shirt.

Experience may come to us directly or indirectly. That is, our experiential base is made up of both real and vicarious experiences. *Real experiences* are those things we have experienced first-hand. *Vicarious experiences* include those from print, movies, television, and other sources we have not experienced first-hand. Vicarious experience is very powerful. One of us has a friend who is a Civil War buff (sometimes known as The War of Northern Aggression among friends from the South). Obviously, he did not directly experience the war. Yet, by reading and seeing movies about it and visiting the battle sites, he has gained great vicarious experience of this conflict. When we read about something that we have not experienced, directly or indirectly, and for which we have no analogous experience, we gain only minimal understanding. One way to view the process of elementary and secondary education is as the careful construction of common experience to serve as the foundation for further learning.

An outline of the discussion to this point would look like this:

PHYSIOLOGICAL
PHONOLOGICAL
UNDERSTANDING
    semantics
    syntax
    experience
       real
       vicarious

Other factors also influence the reading process. They include attitude, purpose, motivation, and attention. For convenience, we will lump together the first three. Actually, we will lump them together because they are in many ways different aspects of similar things. Despite the difficulty in clearly defining where one of these factors ends and the other begins, we will try.

Attitude/Purpose/Motivation

Attitude, purpose, and motivation are treated here as a group of factors each influencing the others and, individually and collectively, exerting an influence on the entire reading process. That influence is easily demonstrated. *Attitude* toward a subject determines, in part, whether the reading will even be attempted and, to some degree, how much will be gained from it. There must be some subject about which every one of us has a negative attitude. If that is true for you, recall for a moment how difficult it was for you to motivate yourself to do the required readings. Perhaps you didn't even do the reading, preferring instead to take your chances. That was the influence of attitude.

Purpose refers to the reason for reading. "What am I supposed to get out of this?" or "Why am I reading this?" are key purpose-related questions.

Purpose can differ greatly from text to text. Recreational reading, for example, has as its purpose, usually never articulated, exactly that: recreation. However, reading an assigned passage without a clear purpose can be very frustrating. For instance, when you are given a quiz and discover that your instructor wanted you to read for detailed information and a high percentage of recall and you read for broad background knowledge, it is a bit too late. Purpose is powerful.

Motivation, influenced by attitude and purpose and influencing the reading process in general, can come from within or without. Some people have great internal motivation. They simply want to do well, whatever they do. Others of us are not so fortunate. We need a payoff—recognition from peers or parents, grades, a pat on the back, money, whatever. The best example of motivation we can think of is from some high school students who, through lack of motivation, rarely do their assigned reading and yet read and study successfully for one particular test: their state's driver's licensing examination. High motivation, a positive attitude, relevant experience, and clear understanding of purpose seem to account for the phenomenon.

Our growing outline of the components of reading should now look like this:

PHYSIOLOGICAL
PHONOLOGICAL   Attitude/Purpose/Motivation
UNDERSTANDING
    semantics
    syntax
    experience
      real
      vicarious

Attitude, purpose, and motivation are set off to one side, out of the general top-to-bottom flow, to indicate that they can facilitate the process at any point or grind it to a dead halt. That is, they can enhance the process, as in the example of the students taking the driver's test, or hamper it, as when we read material from an unfamiliar discipline.

One more component belongs on the side of our outline. It is *attention*. It may seem obvious to the point of being unnecessary that attention must be a part of successful reading. Nevertheless, the component is worth noting for several reasons. First, attention is unidirectional. As much as it would be desirable and even fun to have it be otherwise, we can only direct our attention to one thing at a time. According to Samuels

(Samuels and Kamil, 1984), attention solely to decoding leaves nothing for understanding. That is why incomplete, laborious decoding diminishes or completely destroys understanding. Second, the outward signs of properly directed attention may all be in place and yet result in no understanding. We have all had the experience of dutifully reading an assigned section of text, reaching the end of it, setting the text aside, and realizing we have only the vaguest notion of what it was about. Though our eyes were properly engaged, the words and word order known, our experience useful, and so on, we got nothing out of the reading because our attention was not focused on the reading. It was somewhere else — daydreaming, woolgathering, whatever you choose to call it.

Learning and Change

There is one last component. If everything else is in place and we have successfully read something, there is the possibility that we will have learned something. Since we do not want to engage in a long and probably controversial definition of learning, we will simply say that *learning* here refers to a change in an individual's data base — not merely an addition to it, but a *change* in it. Adding to your store of information through reading means integrating new information with the old, thereby in some sense changing the old, not simply layering new on top of old. An extreme example may serve the point. Many people acknowledge having read a book that changed their lives in big or small ways. No matter whether the book was religious, philosophical, fiction, or fact, it changed their lives because it added to their store of information and thus altered in some more or less profound way much of their previously existing information. Obviously, not everything we successfully read and learn from produces that dramatic a change — but it does produce change. Thus, the last component is:

Learning $\longrightarrow$ Change

(The arrow means "may be rewritten as" or "may be thought of as.") The final outline is shown in Figure 1-1.

In the next section and throughout the book we will refer to this outline. It will serve as the framework for the information, suggestions, and ideas that follow. We hope that you have learned from it in the sense of gaining a new perspective on the reading process.

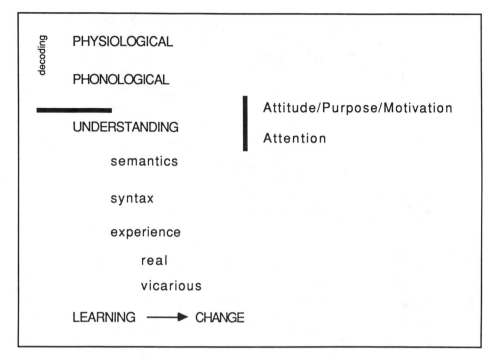

Figure 1-1. Definition of Reading

PREVIEW OF THIS BOOK

Here is a preview of the book's contents and how the various chapters connect to the definition of reading as presented here.

In Chapter 2 we suggest a rationale for introducing your text to your students and a way to do it. The central point of Chapter 2 is that the textbook is the tool of learning that you and your students share. Knowing about that tool and the features it has will help your students become better learners of the subject you teach. Right now, this textbook is the tool you share with your instructor. Its organization is pretty straightforward. There are chapter outlines, chapter introductions, words introduced in boldface or italic print and defined within the context, clearly marked headings and subheadings, and chapter summaries, which are labeled Closing Statements. By using these features, you can get a quick and effective overview of the various chapters. You will find much more about all of this in Chapter 2.

Chapter 3 offers informal and formal ways of predicting read-

ability—or difficulty of reading material—and matching that prediction to students' reading level. It also gives a bit of background on the notion of readability and, most important, provides a perspective on the limitations and pitfalls of readability prediction. Measured readability, it will be noted, does not account well for the influence of prior experience, attitude, purpose, and motivation. We suggest ways to bring those important components into your understanding of texts in each of the succeeding nine chapters.

The vocabulary chapters, Chapters 4 and 5, are based on the premise that knowing the vocabulary of a discipline represents a big step in learning the discipline. Chapter 4 offers ways to use the experience students bring to their textbooks in order to reduce the number of words that you need to teach. Chapter 5 offers efficient, proven techniques for selecting the words to teach, teaching those words, and evaluating the instruction. Vocabulary instruction, whether indirect as in Chapter 4 or direct as in Chapter 5, seems to us a logical subset of comprehension instruction.

The comprehension chapters, Chapters 6 and 7, build on and extend the semantic component of our definition of reading by folding it back into the larger component of understanding. Prereading techniques, including vocabulary instruction and purpose setting, along with an overview of comprehension and questioning techniques, are the topics of Chapter 6. Chapter 7 builds on this with discussion activities and techniques that can serve as either postreading or prereading activities.

Chapters 8 and 9, the writing chapters, explain and illustrate techniques for using writing to extend and reinforce content reading and learning. You may think it is unusual to find a content area reading book with two chapters on writing. However, we are increasingly aware of the interrelatedness of writing and reading for learning. The chapters are practical and content oriented. In our view, chapters on writing to learn are as integral to a text on content area reading as the topic in the next chapter, study skills.

Chapter 10 incorporates the information from the chapters preceding it and shows how that information can inform your thinking about systematic study skills and which to choose to teach for your particular need.

Chapters 11 and 12 cover evaluation and planning. Although last in the book, they can be thought of as both summary and preview statements. Chapter 11 shows how all components of the definition of reading can suggest directions for evaluation. In a sense, Chapter 12 is the condensed version of this textbook since it reiterates what went before. But it also places the preceding chapters in the framework of the Directed Reading Lesson (DRL). We believe that successful instruction begins with evaluation and planning. However, we place these two chapters last because we feel that without an understanding of what reading is and what its role can be in the content area class, it is too early to describe evaluation and planning.

CLOSING STATEMENT

The definition of reading, as presented in this chapter, guided us in the writing of this book. In a similar vein, we have shown how it can guide you in reading and studying this book.

REFERENCES

ANDERSON, RICHARD C., AND FREEBODY, PETER. "Vocabulary Knowledge." In John T. Guthrie (Ed.), *Comprehension and Teaching: Research Reviews*. Newark, DE: International Reading Association, 1981, pp. 77–117.

ANDERSON, RICHARD C., AND PEARSON, P. DAVID. "A Schema-Theoretic View of Basic Processes in Reading." In P. David Pearson (Ed.), *Handbook of Reading Research*. New York: Longman, 1984, pp. 255–291.

CHOMSKY, CAROL S. *The Acquisition of Syntax in Children from 5 to 10*. Cambridge, MA: MIT Press, 1969.

DAVIS, FREDERICK. "Fundamental Factors of Comprehension in Reading," *Psychometrika*, 9, 1944, 185–197.

DAVIS, FREDERICK. "Research in Comprehension in Reading," *Reading Research Quarterly*, 3, 1968, 499–545.

McKEOWN, MARGARET G., AND CURTIS, MARY E. (EDS.). *The Nature of Vocabulary Acquisition*. Hillsdale, NJ: Lawrence Erlbaum, 1987.

SAMUELS, S. JAY, AND KAMIL, MICHAEL L. "Models of the Reading Process." In P. David Pearson (Ed.), *Handbook of Reading Research*. New York: Longman, 1984, pp. 185–224.

SPILICH, GEORGE J.; VESONDER, GREGG T.; CHIESI, H. L.; AND VOSS, JAMES F. "Text Processing of Domain-Related Information for Individuals with High and Low Domain Knowledge," *Journal of Verbal Learning and Verbal Behavior*, 18, 1979, 275–290.

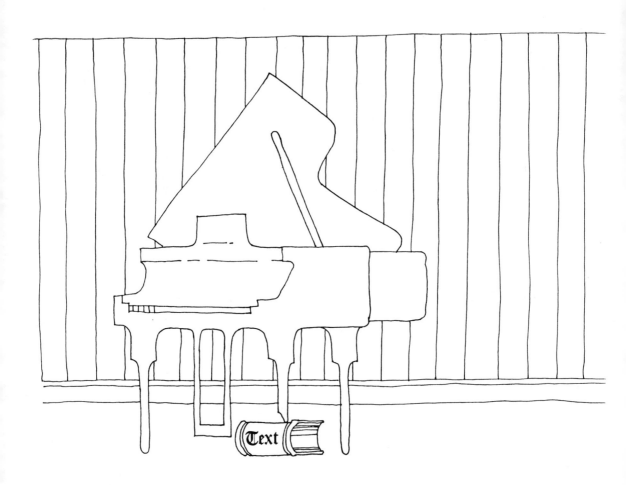

2

TEXT USE

For the vast majority of content teachers, the text they use is the most important of the various tools they have. For the student of whatever discipline is being studied, the text is also the most important tool. And yet, some teachers and many students do not know how to use that tool to its fullest advantage. A text can gather dust from disuse or it can help create the learning environment that you want.

The title of this book is *Content Area Reading: Teachers, Texts, Students*. The "text" is quite deliberately placed between the teacher and the students. The text is the learning tool the teacher and the students use in common. Understanding it and helping your students to understand it means that you and they can then use it more efficiently and more profitably. In this chapter, we discuss the parts of a typical textbook and how you can teach about and use each part.

THE TEXT: WHAT'S IN IT FOR ME?

Good question. Consider this being asked from a teacher's point of view. What is in my text that will help me teach the content of my course to the best of my ability? Notice here that the text is *not* the content, it is an aid to getting the content across to the students. Now consider the same question

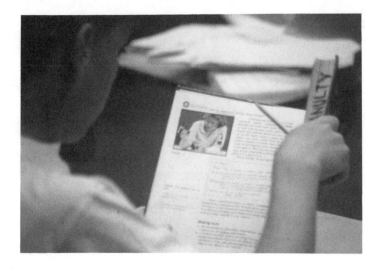

from a student's point of view. What is in my text that will help me learn to the best of my ability the content of this course? Again, the text is an aid— it *represents* the content but *it is not* the content. Combining the two points of view, let us first examine pieces of text and then consider how they can best be used by teacher and student alike. You can decide which parts are important in your textbook for your discipline. Introduce and explain these parts to your students.

PARTS OF A TEXT

Preliminary Pages

Outside Cover.   Starting at the very beginning, the outside cover offers the book title, the name of the publishing company, the author, and frequently some further printed or pictorial information about what is contained in the book.

Title Page.   Immediately inside the cover is the title page. The title page, of course, contains the title of the book. However, it often has a bit more than that. It usually has the author's name and affiliation, which edition it is (if there is more than one), the full name of the publishing company, and the cities where the publishing company maintains offices. This may represent useful information. For example, the author may be one you recognize as important in your field or as representing a particular point of view. If that is the case, you may want to point that out to your students. In addition, the publishing house may have a long and proud history in the field.

Immediately over leaf from the title page is the back of the title page. Really. The technical name is verso title page, which means the back of the title page. (It is also sometimes called the copyright page.) These two pages contain all the publishing information necessary to any bibliographic reference or book order. The verso title page carries the copyright date (or dates if there have been subsequent editions), which is important for several reasons. In some fields, knowledge is growing so rapidly that information may be out of date before the book is even printed. In such fields, a book five or six years old may be nearly useless. In other fields, knowing the date gives important background information, for example with a novel, biography, autobiography, or primary source material in history. If your students pick up the habit of looking at copyright dates, they will gain background knowledge before reading.

Table of Contents. The table of contents is usually next. It can be as sparse as a mere listing of the chapter titles or as elaborate as a listing of all chapters and their headings and subheadings. A gauge of the quality of a table of contents might be whether it, alone, serves as an outline for the entire text. In order to do that, it would have to list, at minimum, the chapter titles and the various major headings within each chapter. On the other hand, a table of contents that is too elaborate loses its utility in an information overload. As is frequently the case, the golden mean is the most desirable.

When first introducing a book to your students, it is well worth the time to peruse the table of contents. It is one of those rare opportunities for a teacher to discuss the full sweep of the course. It should also be an occasion for the teacher and students together to discuss broad purposes, acknowledge prior experience in the field, and generally place in a larger educational perspective the particular course. As will be discussed more fully in the comprehension chapters, knowledge builds on knowledge. The discussion of the broad sweep of a text as it represents a course of instruction is a good way to make that principle clear. You can show students how to scan a table of contents to gain understanding of the book.

Preface. Often, but not always, a preface (or foreword, introduction, or prologue) follows. The preface usually gives a brief preview of the book's content, along with the author's point of view, intent, and purpose for writing. It is best to examine the preface separately and introduce it in terms of what it attempts to do. Teach your students to note an author's bias in the preface and to watch for that bias throughout the book. This can be very important if the author has an unusual interpretation of a scientific process or historical epoch.

Body of the Book

The rest of the book, the body, follows the front matter. Organization will vary considerably from book to book. Examination of a typical chapter format might be helpful in pointing out some of the potentially useful information carried by the format. Please keep in mind that the following discussion is descriptive, not prescriptive. The text you use may or may not have all the elements to be discussed. That does not make it good or bad.

Chapter Introductions or Overviews.   The introduction to a chapter should give a brief overview of what is contained within that chapter. It may be a single paragraph or several pages. It may be in the form of guiding questions or stated as a series of objectives for the chapter. In some texts (as in this one) you will find a mini-table of contents for the chapter or a flowchart, graphical representation, or diagram. These alert the reader to what the author expects the reader to gain from the chapter.

Chapter introductions are useful and usable. Good readers use them to preview a chapter, as we discuss in Chapter 10. You can teach students to pay attention to chapter introductions rather than skipping them as "fluff," because using chapter introductions can make the chapter easier to read and remember.

Chapter Sections.   Within the chapter itself are usually sections on major topics and subsections on subtopics. These sections and subsections are signaled by various typographic cues. For example, in this book sections are signaled by capital bold-faced headings. Subsections are signaled by capital and lower-case bold-faced headings indented from the left margin. If the sections and subsections are well done, a reader should be able to go quickly through a chapter, reading only the section and subsection headings, and get a pretty good feel for what the chapter is about. You can teach students that this tactic, in combination with a careful reading of the introduction, is a good preview technique, as discussed in Chapter 10.

Illustrations.   Illustrations supplement the text and serve to break up and add interest to the text. For example, in a social studies text you might find reproductions of paintings from the era in question or photographs of furniture or homes from that era. When you were in school and got your new books for the year, you very probably examined them for illustrations the first chance you got. You hoped there would be lots of illustrations and there usually were. Your students today are no different. A 400-page history book looks a little less formidable if it is liberally sprinkled with illustrations.

In some cases illustrations are more than supplementary. They are crucial to understanding the text, because they must be understood in order for the text to be understood. Crucial illustrations may include charts, graphs, and tables. The illustrations are typically referred to directly in the text, such as, "See the chart on page 44" or "See Table 1-3." Often, students do not refer to such aids when reading the chapter. You can help by selecting a few that are representative examples from your text or particularly important to your discipline. For example, timelines in history, graphs in economics, and maps in geography are indispensable. Discuss these in class, showing how a chart (or table, graph, or map) relates to and even clarifies the prose.

Vocabulary. In many texts the key vocabulary for the chapter is signaled by typographical cues. Key words and phrases may be in italics, in bold-faced print, underlined, or even in different color print. Textbook authors and publishers know how important it is to signal vocabulary words that are crucial to the discipline. In this text, we highlight vocabulary words in bold-face print; other words that we wish to stress are set in italic print. In Chapters 4 and 5 we talk at length about what you can do with vocabulary.

Chapter Closing. Many textbooks offer a chapter summary. It is usually similar to the chapter introduction except in the format of "this is what you have read," rather than "this is what you are going to read." In fact, in texts that have no summary but do have an introduction, rereading the introduction after reading the chapter is an effective means of immediate review.

In some cases, chapters are closed with discussion questions. These questions vary in style from rather simple, literal recall to application questions. (For a further discussion of questions and question types, see Chapter 6.) Chapter goals should be reflected in the question posed. For example, the classic pattern for mathematics books is a series of problems. Answering the problems allows students to put into practice what they have just learned. On the other hand, social studies texts typically offer a variety of questions intended to check students' recall and allow them to

think about what they have just read in relation to their own experiences. There is no hard and fast rule for judging the questions at the end of a textbook chapter. However, one important criterion is that the questions posed should reflect the goals, stated or unstated, of the particular chapter.

Sources. Many chapters close with a listing of the sources used in writing the chapter. A good way to judge the contemporaneity of a book (in cases where being current is important) is to check the dates of the sources listed against the copyright date of the book. In editions subsequent to the first, it is not unusual to find no sources newer than three to five years before the publication date of the latest edition. This suggests that changes from previous editions are slight — probably only cosmetic.

Some texts offer sources of further information. Thus, if a student wants or needs more information about some topic, she or he has a good start on finding it. It should be kept in mind, however, that the author has probably listed only broad, general references. In other words, the references may not be the best sources for specific points of information. In many cases, a thorough examination of a given topic would require going beyond what the author has offered.

Back Matter

The material following the last chapter may include an appendix (or more than one), an index, and/or a glossary. Let's consider them one at a time.

Appendixes. Appendixes vary in format, style, and number. In mathematics and science texts they typically include tables of one sort or another. In social studies they may include lists of capital cities, pictures of flags, various maps, timelines, and many other possible things. In literature texts you may find biographical sketches of authors or timelines showing literary periods. The point is that there is really no prescribed list of appendixes; therefore, authors put in what they or their publishers want. Again, the test of quality is whether what is included is usable and used. That is, does what is included seem sensible, given the content of the book, and does the author refer to it in the text? If so, it is worth your time to introduce and discuss the appendixes.

Indexes. A good index is an invaluable aid to the text user. But more than that, skillful use of an index is almost a survival skill. Imagine using a cookbook, a computer reference manual, or any kind of repair manual that has no index.

What makes a good index? It should list all the topics and all the names mentioned in the book, but most importantly, it should cross-reference all those things so the reader is able to locate, for example, all the mentions of fur trading in a social studies book. In addition, related topics should be listed. In the example above, it would be reasonable to expect a cross-reference to mountain men, voyageurs, and so on. Students who know how to use indexes can find a specific bit of information, check back to earlier references to the topic, and pursue related topics. This tremendously useful tool is often only dimly understood by students.

Glossaries. A glossary is essentially a small dictionary tucked into the back of the book. Not all books have them; in fact, in our judgment, far too few books have them. However, the entries in a glossary are different from the entries in a dictionary in that they usually define the word only as it is used in that text. This is both an asset and a liability. It is an asset because it has immediate value; it explains the word in a way that it needs to be explained for the purpose of the book. It is a liability because it defines the word too narrowly. Particularly for words that do have broader or multiple meanings, this may unnecessarily limit the students' understanding of the word. In addition, glossaries rarely carry the etymological information found in a good dictionary. Thus, relationships between and among related words may be less apparent. The rest of the dictionary conventions are sometimes adhered to — guide words, synonym listing, and pronunciation keys. The skills needed to make good use of the glossary are virtually the same as those needed to make good use of a dictionary.

Students in secondary school should have had exposure to those skills. Nonetheless, if you are fortunate enough to have a text that includes a glossary, a quick review of dictionary skills might prove beneficial.

DESIGNING A LESSON ON PARTS OF A TEXT

As you have seen, there is much that goes into a text. Getting the most out of it depends on your knowledge of what is in the text and conveying that to your students. The best way to do that is directly. Teach them. Using as your guide the preceding discussion and your current text, you can create a text introduction lesson and a worksheet to go with it. In the lesson, introduce the various parts of the text, discuss them with your students, and ask some questions that will allow the students to explore the issues discussed. The worksheet will serve as an assessment of how well the students have learned (and how well you have taught) the essential pieces of the text and provide a bit of practice and reinforcement. Below is a sample of what might be included in such a lesson. The statements in italics give the goals of each question.

Sample Book-Use Worksheet

1. What is Chapter 7 about? What topics are discussed in Chapter 7? Where did you find that information?
   Directs students to either the table of contents or to a quick look at chapter organization.

2. What was the author's purpose in writing this book? Where did you find that information? What else did you find there?
   Directs students to the preface.

3. What chapter discusses *Topic X?* Where did you find that information? Where else might you find that information?
   Directs students to the table of contents and/or the index.

4. Skim Chapter 4 as quickly as you can. (To skim, quickly read the chapter's title, section headings and subheadings, and any discussion questions.)
   Directs students to a quick examination of chapter organization, including previews and summaries, and shows them how much they pick up about a chapter in a brief time.

5. On what pages is X discussed? Where did you find that information?
   Directs students to the index for efficiency, but the table of contents may also reveal this.

6. What year was this book published? Where did you find that information? Do you think it is important in this textbook?
   Directs students to the front matter, especially the title page or verso title page. Year of publication may be more or less important, depending on content area.

7. *(A question to direct students to whatever appendix or appendixes might be included.)*

8. *(A question to direct students to important visual aids, such as graphs or charts, might be included.)*

9. What key words are introduced in Chapter 5? How are they introduced and explained? If one of those words is used in another chapter, how might you find that information?
   Directs students to how vocabulary is introduced and, again, to the index. Also, if a glossary exists, students should use it for this question.

CLOSING STATEMENT

Content area textbooks are designed to be as helpful to students as possible. Your students might not believe that, but it is true. Among the things included in texts to aid students are the preface, chapter section and subsection headings, chapter summaries, questions at the end of chapters, indexes, appendixes, and often a glossary. If you think of the text as an aid to teaching—a tool—then it follows that skillful use of that tool by students and teachers alike is essential to learning. And yet, many teachers and students do not have a good understanding of the various parts of their textbooks. Direct instruction is the best solution to the problem. A class period or two spent explaining how to use the text will prove profitable in every classroom.

3

READABILITY

Suppose you have to choose reading material for a unit on the weather. If your choices are a thin paperback with pictures entitled A *Simpleton's Guide to the Weather* and a four-pound tome called *Meteorological Compendium,* your choice might be easy, depending on your students and their grade level. But what if you have two similar looking textbooks?

We can quickly infer that one of the books on weather is easier to read than another, just as we can see that *The Bobbsey Twins at the Seashore* and William Faulkner's *The Hamlet* represent extremes on a scale of readability. It is fairly easy to say that the *Meteorological Compendium* and *The Hamlet* are more difficult to read than the other two books. But when the choices are otherwise similar, as with two detective novels, two newspaper articles, or two ninth-grade algebra textbook chapters, it is more difficult to distinguish which is easier or harder for a particular group of readers, such as the students in your class.

Readability is a way of predicting differences in difficulty of reading material by use of a formula. A readability formula, it is claimed, can predict which book is more appropriate for, say, a tenth-grade audience.

For a time it seemed that readability was not talked about much.

Portions of this chapter appear in Timothy C. Standal, "Computer-Measured Readability Formulas," *Computers in the Schools,* 4, 1987, 123–132.

Now, however, because computers make it so easy to use a readability formula, readability influences publishing, especially in the area of textbooks. Teachers need to know about readability as consumers, because textbooks are routinely put through readability formulas and touted as appropriate for certain grade levels. In this chapter we discuss what a readability formula can do but also why it can be misleading or downright wrong to rely on formulas. (In Chapter 11 we discuss another way to match reader to text.)

READABILITY FORMULAS
AND WHAT THEY MEASURE

The notion of readability has a wonderful and ongoing intuitive appeal: Apply a formula to a passage and determine the difficulty of reading level. However, specifying the nature of the relative easiness or difficulty of a reading passage, especially in quantifiable terms, is an unsure science.

One might argue, for example, that the Bobbsey Twins' sandy adventure is, after all, children's literature and it should, therefore, be easier than Faulkner, which is big S, big L—Serious Literature. That is a good and maybe even potent point, but it gives us nothing we can actually measure by counting. Try to imagine what the seeable, countable differences between the two books might be. Length as measured by number of words? Yes, certainly. Difficulty of the vocabulary used? Yes, probably, but how do we measure the difficulty? We might go to a word frequency list that gives us the relative frequency of each word in a book, but that would be terribly time consuming.

The difficulty or complexity of the words used in a passage seem to be an entirely reasonable index of the passage's potential readability. But how does one decide, in some consistent and systematic way, which are the more or less difficult or complex words?

As you can imagine, there are many potential candidates for factors influencing ease or difficulty of reading. As a general rule, longer words are harder than shorter words, which allows us to get some measure of word difficulty. Longer sentences also seem more complex than shorter ones, as a rule. If this is the case, the problem becomes finding a yardstick to measure sentence complexity. Should we count the number of various kinds of clauses? Should we just count sentence length by the number of words per sentence? Maybe the really important difference is the distance, in words, between the subject and the verb in the sentences. It is very difficult to specify in measurable terms what makes one book easier than another.

Nonetheless, according to Abrams (1981), references to the measurement of readability are traceable to around 900 A.D. when writers used word counts to estimate the difficulty of their own writing. The thought was that the more often a word is used, the more likely it is to be known to the reader. This is, of course, a sort of ancient version of the concept of word frequency which, as you will see, still figures heavily in the vast majority of readability formulas. More recently, the push in the 1920s and 1930s for scientific education encouraged the search for ways to quantify the difficulty of books. This search found several seeable factors that can be counted: *semantic* and *syntactic,* referring to words and sentences. Readability formulas came out of this discovery. Although there are many different formulas, the same two factors appear in virtually every readability formula:

Readability Factors

Semantic
   1. Consult a list of words
         or
   2. Measure word length (in letters or syllables)

Syntactic
   3. Measure sentence length (in words)

Semantic Factors

Semantic factors take one of two forms, both having something to do with word frequency. Therefore, several ways have been found to measure the words or vocabulary used.

First, a readability formula can consult a list of words, such as the Dale List of 3,000 familiar words (Dale and Chall, 1948). Words not appearing on the Dale List are counted as unfamiliar, and the more often such words appear in a passage, the higher the readability level. Each word in a reading passage is considered easy or hard, depending on whether it is on the list.

Second, the semantic factor present in many formulas is based on a measure of word length. Longer words are generally less frequent. That means the syllables or even letters of each word can be counted as a way of estimating frequency.

Syntactic Factors

Syntactic factors refer to the sentences. The most common estimate of sentence complexity is sentence length. Longer sentences are generally seen as harder to read and understand. The number of words can be counted to compute an average sentence length.

Using the Formulas

The general way to apply a readability formula to a book is to select three passages at random, from the beginning, middle, and end, to have a representative sample. Count off 100 words and mark off the passage. If the formula you are using asks you to count syllables instead of words, put your hand under your chin; if your head moves when you say the word, count each movement as an extra syllable. Put a tick for the extra syllable and add the extras to a hundred. Calculate the average sentence length. Then refer to a chart for a readability formula. The chart shows the grade level of your reading passage.

We have reproduced the Fry (1977) readability formula in Figure 3-1. We chose this readability formula because it is easy to use and is the most commonly used. For an idea of how it works, follow the seven steps and try the formula on passages.

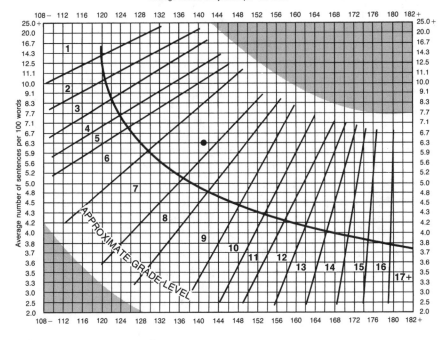

Average number of syllables per 100 words

Expanded Directions for Working Readability Graph

1. Randomly select three (3) sample passages and count out exactly 100 words each, beginning with the beginning of a sentence. Do count proper nouns, initializations, and numerals.
2. Count the number of sentences in the hundred words, estimating length of the fraction of the last sentence to the nearest one-tenth.
3. Count the total number of syllables in the 100-word passage. If you don't have a hand counter available, an easy way is to simply put a mark above every syllable over one in each word, then when you get to the end of the passage, count the number of marks and add 100. Small calculators can also be used as counters by pushing numeral 1, then push the + sign for each word or syllable when counting.
4. Enter graph with *average* sentence length and *average* number of syllables; plot dot where the two lines intersect. Area where dot is plotted will give you the approximate grade level.
5. If a great deal of variability is found in syllable count or sentence count, putting more samples into the average is desirable.
6. A word is defined as a group of symbols with a space on either side; thus, *Joe, IRA, 1945,* and & are each one word.
7. A syllable is defined as a phonetic syllable. Generally, there are as many syllables as vowel sounds. For example, *stopped* is one syllable and *wanted* is two syllables. When counting syllables for numerals and initializations, count one syllable for each symbol. For example, *1945* is four syllables, *IRA* is three syllables, and & is one syllable.

Figure 3–1.   Fry Graph for Estimating Readability—Extended (*Source:* Edward Fry, "Fry's Readability Graph: Clarifications, Validity, and Extension to Level 17," *Journal of Reading,* 21 (1977): 242–252. Reproduction permitted—no copyright.)

Criticisms of Readability Formulas

If you apply readability formulas to texts, fiction, newspapers, *TV Guide*, and the like, you'll find some surprises. The difficulty of "Dear Abby" might fluctuate from day to day. For one thing, different people write the letters. For another, the subject—and therefore the vocabulary difficulty—varies considerably.

Basing readability on word length has its problems. The words *dinosaur* and *hippopotamus* will increase the readability of a first grader's story. Repetition of one long word, such as *constitution* or *photosynthesis* might add to the readability level, depending on the formula. In reality, however, the repetition of a word should make the passage easier to understand, particularly when the word is a central idea of the passage.

Sentence length is not a foolproof method for predicting difficulty of reading either. Shakespeare can come out at a seventh-grade level because readability formulas interpret verse writing as short sentences. Weighty statements such as "I think therefore I am" appear easy to read. As we pointed out in Chapter 1, ease of decoding is not synonymous with comprehension.

In addition, the length of sentences does not account for the connections made between parts. For example, in the two sentences below (after Pearson, 1974–1975), the connectors can make the sentences easier or more difficult to understand in a cause/effect relationship.

Cause			*Effect*	*Example*
x.			y.	John was lazy. He slept late.
x	,		y.	John was lazy, he slept late.
x	,	so	y.	John was lazy, so he slept late.
Because x,			y.	Because John was lazy, he slept late.

Two simple sentences would receive the easiest readability score, whereas the "Because X, Y" form would score as more difficult due to the longer word *because* and the longer sentence. Nevertheless, even though it is longer and has a longer word, the sentence, "Because John was lazy, he slept late" eases our burden of inference by giving us the clearest insight into the cause/effect relationship between John's nature and his behavior.

Thus, we can see that although readability formulas measure two factors, semantic and syntactic, they cannot accurately measure the difficulty of a text.

What Readability Formulas Do Not Measure

In addition to imprecision about semantic and syntactic measurement, readability formulas do not measure other factors of importance in reading. The astute reader will remember the definition of reading from Chapter 1, reproduced here in Figure 3-2. The words *semantics* and *syntax* appear in the definition, but so do *experience, attitude, purpose, motivation,* and *attention.* Readability formulas cannot measure any of the latter qualities of a reading material.

Therefore, word and sentence length are not the *only* factors that contribute to difficulty. Text and reader attributes can (and do) interact in ways that render readability information invalid. For example, Standal

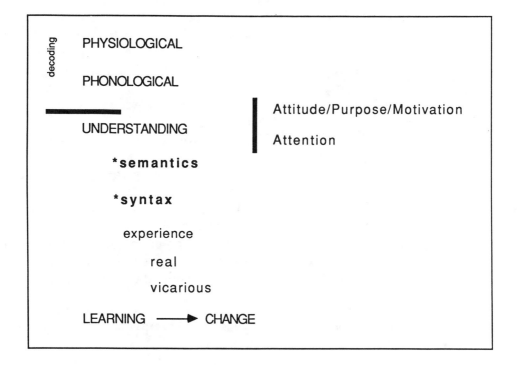

Figure 3-2. Definition of Reading

*Used in readability formulas.

(1978) says prior experience of the reader, reader interest in the topic, and reader motivation for the topic are weighed neither in readability formulas nor in the tests used to determine reader skill level. For all of these reasons and perhaps others, readability formulas are, to some greater or lesser degree, suspect.

As we can see from the definition of reading, just as we can attempt to measure the reading material, so can we attempt to measure qualities about the reader, such as experience and attention. In Chapter 11 we suggest ways to measure these, but our measures of reader skill level are not sufficiently sophisticated to allow precise matching of reader to text.

All that readability formulas claim to do is predict difficulty. However, they *cannot* measure difficulty because they do not nor cannot count the right things — the reader's experience, motivation, attitude, and purpose.

Also, after about eighth or ninth grade, readability predictions will not mean much. Newspapers tend to be written at around an eighth-grade level, but they are not always appropriate for eighth graders. Particularly for secondary readers and older, the background and interest level can be as important as any measure of reading complexity. Given the identical characteristics of syntax and semantics, resulting in an identical readability level, we can recommend particular books on the following topics at a tenth-grade level, but common sense tells us that our individual students will find vast differences in difficulty in books on computer programming, historical novels, engine repair, kayaking techniques, or heavy metal bands. The difficulty will come as much from their knowledge and interest as from the quality of writing in the books themselves.

In addition, some textbooks go to greater lengths than others to make links between concepts and chapters and to refer to concepts throughout, rather than bring them up and drop them. Readability formulas cannot measure this linkage.

A final point worth mentioning is that the preparers of commercially available programs and publishers of textbooks are not always terribly forthcoming about the specifics of their programs. It is possible to run three different programs on the same text, resulting in three different reading levels, and to report the one most suited to the target grade level.

What Readability Formulas Do Measure

Lest we discard readability formulas completely, we should remember that the closer we can match a textbook with our students' levels of reading ability, the more success we will have in using the text as a teaching tool. Whereas the factors of semantics and syntax alone cannot predict reading level with entire accuracy, neither can any other single factor predict reading success.

For example, one of us observed a social studies lesson with academically disenchanted students at an alternative high school. Because of their personal interest in the subject, they had been given an article to read on drugs. That is, the teacher chose the article based on the students' attitude, motivation, and experience. The article, however, came from the highly articulate *National Review.* Had a readability formula been applied to the article, it would have shown that regardless of the match in interest, the difficulty level of the article was far too high for these students. The lesson was a flop; the students could not read the article. They experienced an unnecessary failure with reading.

The criticisms of readability formulas are unarguably important, but their power as points of criticism is blunted a good bit if one considers readability formulas as *predictors* of readability rather than as *measures* of readability, as Klare (1984) suggests. The following example illustrates this distinction. Given enough experience, we can probably *predict* with a fair degree of accuracy how long it will take to ride a bicycle a certain distance over a certain kind of terrain. However, *measuring* that event can only take place during and after the event. The same is true for text. We can *predict,* by use of formulas, the readability of a certain text for a certain person of a certain skill level, but we can *measure* it only during and after a real person has read a given passage. The distinction between predicting the readability of text and measuring the readability of text is a good one to keep in mind.

CLOSING STATEMENT

It seems likely that the number of readability programs will increase along with the growth in the availability and use of microcomputers, thereby becoming less expensive and increasingly common.

These formulas were certainly given new life in their computerized versions. What had been tedious, time-consuming, and, therefore, rarely or poorly done work became, instead, easy, quick, and efficient. It is now not uncommon to find whole school districts that routinely compute the readability levels of all their textbooks.

Unfortunately, formulas are being misused as prescriptive, rather than descriptive. That means material can be and is rewritten to a formula (rather than to the content of the book or to the background or interest of the readers).

Since there are now so many readability analyses done routinely by so many school clerical personnel, the classroom teacher (and other education professionals) is increasingly distant from the process (Schlick Noe and Standal, 1984–1985). This means that she or he does not know how the text was sampled, whether the proper program was used, and whether the program was properly run.

Readability measurement with all its pitfalls is not going to go away, and — assuming a well-informed population of users — that may not be such a bad thing. Certainly, readability formulas as predictors of difficulty do a remarkably good job. But problems arise when formulas with their numbers and computer programs gain an "aura of precision" (Duffelmeyer, 1985) such that they are taken as more meaningful than they really are.

If you think you have a great text but its readability is high, use it; be suspicious of the readability formula alone. Readability formulas are predictors of difficulty, not measures of difficulty, and if used in combination with good professional judgment and common sense, they do just that — predict difficulty level. Be wary of their accuracy and use them as a starting point. A readability formula used in combination with teacher experience and common sense provides a good general predictor of text appropriateness — no more and no less.

REFERENCES

ABRAMS, MARIE J. "Readability: Its Use in Adult Education," *Lifelong Learning*, 4, 1981, 8–9.

DALE, EDGAR, AND CHALL, JEANNE S. "A Formula for Predicting Readability," *Educational Research Bulletin*, 28, 1948, 11–20.

DUFFELMEYER, F. "Estimating Readability with a Computer: Beware the Aura of Precision," *The Reading Teacher*, 38, 1985, 392–394.

FRY, EDWARD. "Fry's Readability Graph: Clarifications, Validity, and Extension to Level

17," *Journal of Reading*, 21, 1977, 242–252.

KLARE, GEORGE R. "Readability." In P. D. Pearson, R. Barr, M. Kamil, and P. Mosenthal (Eds.), *Handbook of Reading Research*. New York: Longman, 1984, pp. 681–744.

PEARSON, P. DAVID. "The Effects of Grammatical Complexity on Children's Comprehension, Recall, and Conception of Certain Semantic Relations," *Reading Research Quarterly*, 10, 1974–1975, 155–192.

SCHLICK NOE, KATHERINE, AND STANDAL, TIMOTHY C. "Computer Applications of Readability Formulas: Some Cautions," *Computers in Reading and the Language Arts*, 2, 1984–1985, 16–17, 43.

STANDAL, TIMOTHY C. "Readability Formulas: What's Out, What's In?" *The Reading Teacher*, 21, 1978, 642–646.

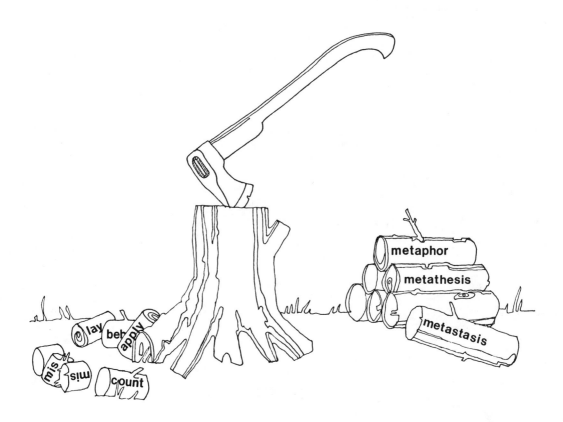

4

VOCABULARY: REDUCING THE NEED TO TEACH

When we say a person is a biologist, a historian, or a sociologist, we mean, in part, that she or he understands the language and the structure of the discipline named. To a great extent, the language and the structure of the discipline are inseparable since the words used are the labels for concepts and concepts are the stuff of the structure. Therefore, to really know the language of a discipline is, in large measure, to know the discipline.

Oftentimes students (and others) reject the words used within a discipline as mere jargon. Indeed, the universal human proclivity for special words does, in many cases, make discipline-specific vocabulary seem a transparent attempt to keep the ins in and the outs out. Nonetheless, such "special words" (and abbreviations, although even we think this is getting a bit out of hand) serve the function of precision. A simple example may serve to aid the argument.

Take the word *line*. What does it mean? Well, you say, that depends. And on what it depends is how it is used, by whom, in what context, in what environment. Let's try some different possibilities.

1. A poet discussing his or her work with another poet

2. A mathematician discussing her or his work in geometry with another mathematician

3. A Las Vegas gambler placing a bet on a sporting event

4. A person discussing fishing with another person

5. A person overhearing the initial conversation between two people in a singles bar

6. A reporter seeking additional information for a story

There are, we are sure, many other possibilities. Still, the point is made. Each of these activities has some specialized meaning for the word *line*.

Within every discipline—within every activity humans engage in, for that matter—there is a specialized vocabulary that may be thought of as the language of that discipline. That language may be further thought of as having two components: words unique to that discipline and general words that have specific meanings unique to that discipline. Vacca and Vacca (1986) refer to these categories as *technical* and *special,* respectively. The word *line,* as previously used in any one of the contexts given, is an example of a special word. Its general meaning is greatly modified or set aside entirely in favor of the precise meaning needed for a particular context. And, one more time, knowing and understanding the language of a discipline represents a big step toward understanding the discipline itself.

Knowing a word means that you can recognize it when you see it or hear it, or it may mean that you can produce it in your speech or in your writing. Why the distinction?

Recognition is easier. The word is in front of the student rather than in the student's memory, and it is surrounded by context. It is amenable to contextual and structural analysis if it is in print. Recognition is always easier than production. Recognizing your friends is much easier than describing them to someone else. If you are confident that students will encounter a word only in a spoken or written context, you should teach those words for recognition. After all, the need to know is restricted to recognition.

Production, on the other hand, is harder, with a greater—or at least more noticeable—risk of being wrong. Words that are produced in writing need to be spelled correctly. Production also requires the appropriate use of various forms of the word depending on how it is used. It should be noted that production subsumes recognition. If you can choose it and use it correctly, you can also recognize it.

Selecting and teaching the words necessary to understand a given discipline are the proper jobs of the content area teacher. The job of teaching vocabulary may seem a very big one. It is. Nevertheless, good planning makes the job less daunting. First, it is not your job to teach vocabulary indiscriminately. Vocabulary instruction is a tool that you use for teaching the content of your discipline. By selecting vocabulary according to your purpose, you reduce the number of words that you need to teach, and you make the instruction more meaningful because the words are unified by a purpose. Second, you can further reduce the amount of time you spend in direct vocabulary instruction by using what students already know about deriving meaning from context and the parts of words. Instead of discussing direct vocabulary instruction here, we leave that topic to Chapter 5. In this chapter we discuss how you can reduce the need to teach vocabulary by carefully selecting the vocabulary and by taking advantage of students' knowledge of context and parts of words.

SOURCES FOR LEARNING VOCABULARY

It may seem odd to subtitle a vocabulary chapter "Reducing the Need to Teach," but we believe that is the place to begin. Why? Because your goal as a content teacher is not one of global vocabulary expansion. Rather, it is to provide for students an understanding of the words necessary to their study of your discipline. A good way to begin that process is by taking advantage of what your students already know. And what they already know is a great deal about their language and how it is used.

According to Burmeister (1975), when fluent readers read they generally recognize nearly all the words they come in contact with immediately, *at sight* (see Figure 4–1). If they do not, they generally examine the *context* in which the word appears in order to get an idea of what the word means. If that does not help, they move to an examination of the word's

As fluent readers we recognize most words **at sight:**

cat, SONY, My name is Suzie M.

But if we don't, we try the **context:**

She broke her neck when she *dove* into the pool.
The *dove* cooed and walked the city streets.

or

He fell *down.*
The computer is *down.*
She felt *down* today.
They stuffed it with goose *down.*

If that doesn't work, we try analyzing the **parts of a word** (called structural or morphological analysis):

psych*ology,* soci*ology,* music*ology:* "-ology" means the study of.
*eco*system, *eco*nomic: "eco-" means habitat or environment.

Sometimes that still doesn't work. You may know that "cracy" relates to government and "pluto" to the Saturday cartoons and therefore be unable to derive plutocracy (a government run by the wealthy). Then, we try matching our knowledge of sounds to letters, called *phonics:*

slide, hand, monosodiumglutamate

If all else fails, we put out the SOS, *some other source* (the dictionary, a teacher, a friend):

"Hey, Grandma, what does 'holy cow' mean?"

Figure 4–1. Steps Used by Fluent Readers (Adapted from Burmeister, 1975)

parts (called *structural analysis* or morphological analysis) to see if there are word parts that might give them hints about the word's meaning. These parts might be root words, as in *photo*, meaning light, and *graph*, meaning writing. Thus, a *photograph* is what the light writes on the film. If that proves of no help, fluent readers may then use their *phonic* skills in order to pronounce the word. This, presumably, is done in the hope that hearing the word will spark recognition. If that fails, they turn to the *dictionary* or some other source (SOS). The other source oftentimes is the teacher or some other student, if our reader happens to be in school.

You have no doubt experienced this hierarchy yourself. You are somewhere, minding your own business, when a friend says, "Hey, what does this word mean?" If you don't know right off (sight), you say, "Read me the sentence" (context). If you still do not know, you may speculate about parts of the word you recognize (structural analysis), then pronounce it, to yourself or aloud, to see if anything leaps to mind (phonics). If nothing does, you no doubt admit defeat and suggest to your friend that she or he "look it up." Although you have been no help whatsoever to your friend, you have demonstrated the process most of us go through.

Obviously, readers do not go through Burmeister's hierarchy of meaning-getting in discrete stages. That is, they do not (and probably could not if they wanted to) separate context from structural analysis or sounding it out. Although we do not always go through these steps in this order, most of us use them. Table 4–1 shows each component and what it may provide to the reader stumped by a word she or he has come across in reading. Some students go too early to SOS—meaning you.

The Burmeister hierarchy of word attack skills provides an explanation and rationale for the discussion in this chapter on reducing the need to

Table 4.1   Hierarchy of Word Attack Skills (after Burmeister, 1975)

Hierachy	*Does it help with PRONUNCIATION?*	*Does it help with MEANING?*
SIGHT	Yes	Yes
CONTEXT	Not Necessarily	Approximately
STRUCTURAL ANALYSIS	Not Necessarily	Approximately
PHONICS	Yes	No
DICTIONARY	Yes*	Yes*

*Assuming requisite dictionary skills.

teach vocabulary. Each component of the hierarchy has a notation about whether it contributes to pronunciation and/or understanding.

Skillful users of context and structural analysis—and we are all skilled to some degree—need less direct instruction in vocabulary. Thus, the time you spend in class sharpening these skills pays off in greater ease of reading for your students and in reduction of your time spent in direct vocabulary instruction.

Using Context as a Tool

In Chapter 2 we noted that many texts carefully introduce new words by highlighting them (bold-face print, color, underlining, italics, etc.) and placing them in rich context. For example, we can guess the meaning of *purebred* from the context of this sentence in a biology test (Slesnick, Balzer, McCormack, Newton, and Rasmussen, 1985):

Pea plants that inherit an allele for red flower color from each parent will be a pure strain, or **purebred,** for red flower color.

Textbook writers and publishers know how powerful context is. So should your students. They can, in effect, instruct themselves by using context to figure out a word's meaning. Textbooks deliberately place unknown words in rich context. For instance, the word *allele*, in the example just cited, was in the paragraph preceding the one quoted. With this rich context, students have an easier time learning and using the skill. Here is how. Examine a textbook in your subject area to see how vocabulary is introduced. You will find that some combination or all of the clue types listed and explained below are used. Teaching your students to use these clues in their texts goes a long way toward reducing the need to teach vocabulary. In fact, where a word is defined in the text and in cases where students have been taught to use the information the text gives, such words need not be taught directly. Your students are independent from SOS, and your time is freed for other teaching. Words defined in the text should be thought of as accessible through context.

Instruction in deriving a word's meaning from the direct context-clue types used in your text is a logical follow-up to the text introduction lesson. However, such instruction requires consistent use and reinforcement. So, in constructing vocabulary lessons, you might wish to list separately the words that are essential to your **purpose** for a given reading assignment but which are accessible from context.

There are many possible categories for context clues. For our purposes we will consider that there are five, which are defined and illustrated here.

1. Definition: A word is used and a short definition, set off by commas, is included. This is what your eighth-grade English teacher tried desperately to teach you is a phrase in apposition.
   Example:
   Mycology, the branch of botany dealing with fungi, is of great interest to mushroom hunters.

2. Synonym: Very similar to the above except that a familiar word that is synonymous or nearly synonymous is used. The same English teacher called this a word in apposition.
   Example:
   The production of *porcine* animals, hogs, is very important to the economies of several midwestern states.

3. Comparison or Contrast: The word in question is compared to or contrasted with something the reader is presumed to know.
   Example:
   The food served in the various chain restaurants along interstate highways is seldom, if ever, mistaken for *haute cuisine*.

4. Summary: The word or phrase in question is an overarching or superordinate term for a number of things or attributes. It may precede or succeed the subordinate terms.
   Example:
   Murder, rape, and arson would certainly have to be included in any list of *sociopathic* activities while incorrigible overtime parking probably would not.

5. Mood or Tone: The meaning of the word or phrase in question is discernible from the mood or tone of the larger context in which it appears.
   Example:
   With students tumbling out of the buildings shouting their plans and goodbyes for the summer and with teachers a bit more tolerant, perhaps even radiant, it is clear that the *euphoria* of the last day of school affects everyone.

As we noted, there are numerous possible categorization schemes for context clues. The ones listed and illustrated are thought to cover the range of possibilities. And that is the point. For you, and certainly for your students, the number of categories and the names of the categories are not important. What is important is making conscious use of these language aids. That is something any reasonably competent reader can do. In the next section we suggest some possibilities.

Handling the Acquisition, Instruction, and Assessment of Context Clues

Included here is a list of some fairly obvious ways to handle the acquisition, instruction, and assessment of context clues:

1. A reasonably adventurous soul might discuss the clues that we just talked about, give examples, have students produce examples, and then apply the skill in some real reading material. Practicing this skill provides a good opportunity for paired or small group work. One caution, however: Use the categories only as an illustration of the potential ways for context clues to be used. Do not ask your students to "know" the names of the various clues.

2. Create a handout on which the mysterious words have been deleted. Have the students replace the words. (Don't do too many.) When we read we are aided in our understanding of the words used by the context in which the words appear. For example, when a word we might not know is followed by a brief definition enclosed in commas, that is a _____ context clue. If a familiar word enclosed in commas follows a word we might not know, that is a _____ context clue. This activity is a way of sharpening skills that students already have.

3. Follow the procedure in #2 above, but also provide the words and their synonyms. Have students choose from the list. Some younger or less sophisticated readers might need to do this easier activity before they do the more difficult one in #2. This one is recognition, whereas #2 is production.

4. For purposes of assessment, write your own sentences using good strong context clues in order to see how well your students can use this important skill.

5. Ask class members to provide examples of words found in their nonschool reading that they were able to figure out from context. Post the examples.

6. Ask students to help you figure out the precise meaning of some current slang word or phrase by giving several good strong contexts for it. Let them judge whether you've understood.

7. Think of words that have multiple meanings (range, pitch, set, run, home, etc.). Think of nonsense words. Use a nonsense word in place of a word that has many possible meanings in two or three of its more usual meanings. See if students can figure out from the context what real word you had in mind.

8. Write sentences using explanatory phrases in place of target words. Have students substitute the word for the explanatory phrase. If no list is provided, this is a vocabulary production activity. If a list is given, it is a vocabulary recognition activity.

Of course, context is not just context. Beck, McKeown, and Mc-Caslin (1983) argue persuasively for at least four levels of context. The levels depend on the degree to which the context is informative. *Misdirective* context is that which would lead the reader to a wrong, perhaps opposite, definition of the target word. *Nondirective* context is that which does not offer enough for the reader to use in defining the word in question. *General* context is rich enough to give the reader a general notion

of what the word means. Finally, *directive* context is rich to the point of allowing the reasonably sophisticated user of context to come up with a quite good definition of the target word. In addition to these four levels, Beck, McKeown, and McCaslin suggest a fifth category, *pedagogical*, which is akin to directive and is typically found in textbooks. This is the context most likely to follow the patterns established in the context clue types described above. In our discussion of context learning as a way of reducing the need to teach vocabulary, we have in mind directive, pedagogical, and, to a more limited extent, general contexts. The core of our argument is that these richer levels of context are text features that the reader needs to learn to use. The richer levels of context do show up in nontextbook text, but do so less often.

Using Structural Analysis as a Tool

Students probably know much more about the pieces of their language than they realize. For example, the average secondary student probably would understand any short list of common prefixes ("pre-," "in-," "de-") and suffixes ("-ment," "-ology," "-ly"). The same is true for the more common root words, as in our example of *photograph* a few pages back. English has borrowed from many languages—chiefly Latin, French, and Greek. Thus, your task of making students aware of what they already know and of the power of their knowledge is twofold: general experience and knowledge specific to the discipline.

General awareness of structural analysis is best fostered in an informal way. Early in the next chapter you will read a vocabulary instruction principle that states that words are learned from a need or desire to know them. Well, the same is true for affixes and roots. Merely studying them apart from a desire or need is of limited value. What is not of limited value is a lesson or series of lessons designed to remind people of what they already know.

Here are some techniques you can use quickly and easily in the classroom that serve to bring to conscious awareness potentially useful knowledge about structural analysis.

1. Ask students to suggest common word parts. Simply list on the board affixes and roots that students suggest in class. This is a whole-class activity that benefits everyone. The number of words that students come up with

shows them how much they already know and allows them to review parts they do not know.

2. Use a list generated as above or specifically written for this purpose to make up a word. The only rule is that the definition of the made-up word must be consistent with its parts.
    Example:
    The parts in "microverdeanthropology" mean "small," "green," and "the study of people." Therefore, the study of little green people must be the proper concern of microverdeanthropologists.
    "Pneumocranial" comes from two roots meaning "air" and "head," as in, "He seems a bit pneumocranial to me."

3. Attach affixes or roots to current slang words. Rather than dating this book unnecessarily by choosing a current word that would probably be "out" before this is printed, we will use a simple example. "Twit" is a Britishism that means, roughly, a person who is objectionable in some way—socially incompetent, boorish, or generally out of it. From this beginning we can establish hundreds of easily understood terms that might relate to aspects of twitdom (there's one).
    Example:
    Twitology/twitologist—The study of twits.
    Twitogram—The writing of a twit.
    Twitometer—An instrument to measure twits by height, weight, etc.
    Twitophony—The sounds that twits make.
    Twitophonologist—The study of the sounds that twits make.
Pre-twit, untwit, retwit, twitted, twitting, and more—The possibilities are endless.

4. Find the use of affixes and roots in product names or in made-up adjectives for various products. For example, the prescription drug "librium" is so named for its roots which suggest both balance and freedom.

5. Identify the most common word parts in your discipline. Within the study of virtually every discipline some affixes and roots are frequent and relatively invariant in meaning. Learning, consciously learning, a fairly small number of these can unlock hundreds of words. There are several ways to approach this task. First, however, you must identify the target affixes and roots. Do this by previewing your text and noting likely candidates. Those identified can then be included in activities such as those above or included in regular vocabulary lessons with special attention to recurring pieces. Examples are all of the "-archy" and -ocracy" words used in social studies, such as *democracy, autocracy, monarchy, anarchy,* and so on. Exam-

ples in mathematics are all of the number words such as *mono, duo,* and *quadra.*

Again, the point of these activities is to help make students aware of how much they already know. These kinds of activities are consciously included in the classroom but are short in duration and informal in style. Evaluation is probably unwise and uninformative.

CHOOSING THE WORDS TO TEACH

Before we move on to the issue of direct vocabulary instruction, we must consider the most crucial aspect of vocabulary instruction in a content area class: How do you choose the words? We've seen as many as thirty vocabulary words listed in the front of chapters, which seemed to us a dauntingly long list, and we've also seen words chosen at random, for all the logic we could detect behind their choice.

Ask yourself: What is my purpose in assigning this reading? What do I want my students to get out of it? In deciding which words to teach for a given lesson, it is useful to consider the questions of centrality and utility. *Centrality* means that the word or words are central, crucial, to the purpose for which the reading is being done. *Utility* means that the word or words are likely to be needed and used beyond the lesson at hand.

Take as an example the word *tack,* as it refers to saddles, bridles, and such used in riding horses. First, you should notice that this is a special word. It has a more general meaning aside from this special context. Second, it may represent a new label for an old concept, at least for older students. That is, it is a superordinate label for various items with which the students may be more or less familiar. Now, consider the word *tack* in these possible contexts.

In a social studies chapter on the cattle drives in the Old West, *tack* appears in the following context: "The cowboys were responsible for selecting their own horses from those provided but they had to use their own tack." Is this word central to the purpose for which this chapter is being read? It seems unlikely. Is it highly useful beyond this context? Again, it seems unlikely. This, then, becomes a word worth mentioning perhaps but not worth teaching.

Consider another possibility. In your Language Arts class you are reading a realistic novel about a girl's life on a ranch in Wyoming in the early part of this century. A good part of the heroine's chores consist of caring for the tackroom and the tack therein. She is responsible for keeping it in good repair. One of the hands is badly hurt when the saddle cinch breaks, and of course the heroine is blamed. The central conflict of the story is her concern for the rider who was hurt and her desire to redeem herself by proving that she was not negligible. (Maybe there is an evil, land-grabbing rancher next door who is really responsible. Who can say?) Does the word *tack* become central to the story? Of course it does. Does it become highly useful? Yes and no. Yes, in that it is likely to appear frequently as the story progresses, but no in that its appearance beyond this story is not likely. What to do? Teach for recognition. That will satisfy the immediate need and purpose.

Once you've chosen the central words, decide which you need to instruct directly. As an example, chapter 5, section 1 of *Civics: Citizens in Action* (Turner, Long, Bowes, and Lott, 1986) is entitled "Becoming an American Citizen." As the title clearly suggests, the section is about the various ways in which people become U.S. citizens. For purposes of this discussion, we will answer the above purpose-setting questions this way. (The class is seventh-grade social studies.) We want our students to have a basic understanding of U.S. citizenship, how one gains it, who gains it, and how it may be lost or given up. Our plan is that these issues will be explored in a classroom discussion and tied to the contemporary issue of illegal aliens. The reading will be introduced and the vocabulary taught in one class session and the discussion will take up the following class period. With that purpose in mind, we have identified the following terms from the seven-page section:

Law of the Soil	immigrant*
Law of Blood	quota*
petition*	nationals*
assimilated*	aliens*
refugees*	illegal aliens*
expatriation*	visa*
naturalization*	deportation*
denaturalization*	

(Turner, Long, Bowes, and Lott, 1986)

That may look like a daunting list, especially for one lesson's read-ing. It is. However, the asterisked terms appear in bold-face print in the text and are defined in the text. Since our students have been taught to use their text aids and, more specifically, have been taught to use context clues and morphological analysis, the only terms we must teach directly are "Law of the Soil" and "Law of Blood." We will list all the other terms as crucial to our reading purpose and accessible through context study and analysis of words parts.

Here, for example, is the text's treatment of the word *refugee*, which allows the students to gain meaning of the word through context clues:

> Thousands of "special immigrants" also come to the United States each year. **Refugees,** or people who leave their own country for protection and safety, are part of this group (Turner, Long, Bowes, and Lott, 1986, p. 106).

Notice also that some words are amenable to morphological analysis, especially *expatriation, naturalization,* and *denaturalization.*

Referring to our civics example above, since we intend to have the words in context in front of the students during the discussion and since these are discipline-specific words, we intend to teach for recognition, not production. (Note: This does not mean that the students will not produce the words in the discussion. They will. It just means that they are not expected to do so without relevant and available context.)

We can think of word knowledge as existing along a continuum from none to full knowledge (see Figure 4–2). Using our earlier terms, *recognition* and *production,* you can see that recognition is called for in the lower half of the continuum and production is called for in the upper half. If you factor in the notion of "need," as suggested in the vocabulary acquisition principle that is discussed in Chapter 5, this continuum should help you better conceptualize the goals of your own vocabulary instruction. Returning to our own examples from the civics book, we suggest that the two terms to be taught, "Law of Blood" and "Law of the Soil," be taught for recognition. Remember, recognition means that students understand a word when they see or hear it, whereas production means that students can use the word in writing and speaking. We further suggest that the students' knowledge of these terms, assuming a well-taught and well-learned lesson, would be at about the .4 level on the proposed word knowledge continuum in Figure 4–2. That is the extent of the need for these two terms. Words

PERFECT
KNOWLEDGE

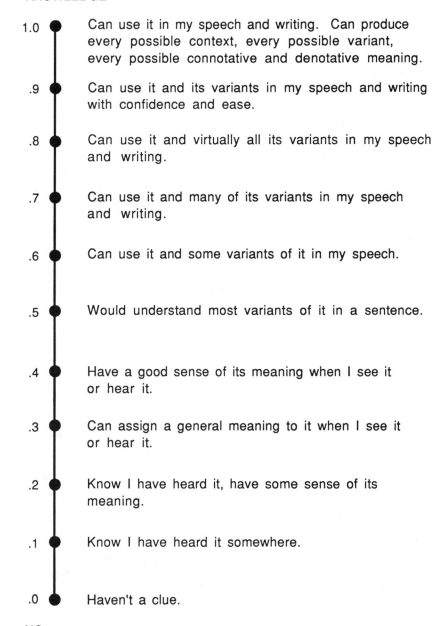

1.0   Can use it in my speech and writing. Can produce
       every possible context, every possible variant,
       every possible connotative and denotative meaning.

.9   Can use it and its variants in my speech and writing
       with confidence and ease.

.8   Can use it and virtually all its variants in my speech
       and writing.

.7   Can use it and many of its variants in my speech
       and writing.

.6   Can use it and some variants of it in my speech.

.5   Would understand most variants of it in a sentence.

.4   Have a good sense of its meaning when I see it
       or hear it.

.3   Can assign a general meaning to it when I see it
       or hear it.

.2   Know I have heard it, have some sense of its
       meaning.

.1   Know I have heard it somewhere.

.0   Haven't a clue.

NO
KNOWLEDGE

Figure 4-2. Proposed Word Knowledge Continuum

that you deem essential for talking or writing about your discipline should be taught for production.

CLOSING STATEMENT

This chapter has dealt with the planning and instruction issues that precede direct instruction in vocabulary. Instruction in the use of contextual and morphemic analysis, it has been suggested, reduces the need for direct instruction of vocabulary. By helping make your students more independent with vocabulary, you gain more classroom time to spend on the most important vocabulary in your discipline. Planning for instruction means choosing the words to teach based on purpose for reading, that is, choosing words that are central to understanding the material to be read. In addition, having some sense of what those words may represent to the students in terms of the concept and label gives you an idea of how to plan the instruction. The next chapter presents techniques for directly teaching vocabulary.

REFERENCES

BECK, ISABEL L.; MCKEOWN, MARGARET G.; AND MCCASLIN, ELLEN S. "All Contexts Are Not Created Equal," *Elementary School Journal*, 83, 1983, 177–181.

BURMEISTER, LOU E. *Words—From Print to Meaning*. Reading, MA: Addison-Wesley, 1975.

CARNINE, DOUGLAS W.; KAMENNUI, EDWARD J.; AND COYLE, GAYLE. "Utilization of Contextual Information in Determining the Meaning of Unfamiliar Words," *Reading Research Quarterly*, 19, 1984, 188–204.

EEDS, MARYANN, AND COCKRUM, WARD A. "Teaching Word Meanings by Expanding Schemata vs. Dictionary Work vs. Reading in Context," *Journal of Reading*, 28, 1985, 492–497.

GRAVES, MICHAEL F. "The Roles of Instruction in Fostering Vocabulary Development." In Margaret G. McKeown and Mary E. Curtis (Eds.), *The Nature of Vocabulary Acquisition*. Hillsdale, NJ: Lawrence Erlbaum, 1987, pp. 165–184.

NAGY, WILLIAM E.; HERMAN, PATRICIA A.; AND ANDERSON, RICHARD C. "Learning Words from Context," *Reading Research Quarterly*, 20, 1985, 233–253.

SCHATZ, ELINORE K., AND BALDWIN, R. SCOTT. "Context Clues Are Unreliable Predictors of Word Meanings," *Reading Research Quarterly*, 21, 1986, 439–452.

SLESNICK, IRWIN L.; BALZER, LEVON; MCCORMACK, ALAN J.; NEWTON, DAVID E.; AND RASMUSSEN, FREDERICK A. *Biology*. Glenview, IL: Scott, Foresman, 1985.

STERNBERG, ROBERT J. "Most Vocabulary Is

Learned From Context." In Margaret G. McKeown and Mary E. Curtis (Eds.), *The Nature of Vocabulary Acquisition.* Hillsdale, NJ: Lawrence Erlbaum, 1987, pp. 89–105.

TURNER, MARY JANE; LONG, CATHRYN J.; BOWES, JOHN S.; AND LOTT, ELIZABETH J. *Civics: Citizens in Action.* Columbus, OH: Charles E. Merrill, 1986.

VACCA, RICHARD T., AND VACCA, JO ANNE L. *Content Area Reading,* 2nd ed. Boston: Little, Brown, 1986.

5

TEACHING VOCABULARY DIRECTLY

First of all, a guiding principle: *People learn only the words they need to know or want to know and they learn them to the depth needed or wanted.* A simple example will suffice here. Probably at some point in your school career you were given the following assignment: "Look up these twenty words, write out the definition for each and use the word in a sentence. Due Thursday; quiz on Friday." If you were given one such assignment, you were given many. Chances are that you recall none of the words or their meanings. If you do recall one or more of the words you met in this fashion, it is most likely it or they had some special attraction for you. You liked the sound. You had come across it in your personal reading and wanted to know its meaning. You heard it used. The point is that out of those potentially hundreds of words, you may remember none or only a very small number that were, for some reason, special to you. People learn only the words they need to know or want to know and they learn them to the depth needed or wanted. This leads to the principle of vocabulary instruction: *Teach people only the words they need to know or want to know and teach them to the depth needed or wanted.*

This principle of vocabulary instruction is simply another way of saying that there is no point in trying to teach people words that they don't need or want. We hope that doesn't sound terribly bleak. It shouldn't.

There is nothing in it that suggests you can't create and exploit (in the nicest sense of the word) the need and desire to know.

Consider what the words you have chosen to teach may represent to your students—the "experience" element in our definition of reading in Chapter 1. There are four possibilities, as shown in Figure 5-1.

Since words are labels for concepts, the possibilities are:

Both label and concept known. This, of course, represents the students' extant vocabulary. These are the words and concepts they know—or at least know to the depth needed for your purposes. Let us use the word *heart* as it appears in the phrase "affairs of the heart." This is unlikely to cause any problem for older students. Both label and concept are known.

Label known but concept unknown. This represents what was earlier referred to as "special" vocabulary. That is, a new and/or more precise use

	Label	
	Known	Unknown
Concept Known	Word is in present vocabulary.	Word requires learning a new label for something already known.
Concept Unknown	Word requires learning a concept or a new use for an old label or both.	Word requires learning a new label and a new concept.

Figure 5-1. Relationship of Labels and Concepts (after Jenkins and Dixon, 1983)

of a previously known word (label). Let us again take as our example the word *heart,* but now as it might be used in a health book. This, then, is not the *heart* of Valentine's Day.

Label unknown but concept known.   Much of foreign language teaching falls into this realm, but we also increase our vocabulary by adding new labels to concepts already known. For example, your students might know what a "horse shoer" is but not a "farrier." Therefore, they need only to learn the word. In principle, learning labels for known concepts should be easy, if the principle of vocabulary instruction is adhered to.

Both label and concept unknown.   Into this category falls much specialized vocabulary crucial for a discipline. Depending on a student's background knowledge, examples might be *photosynthesis, matrix algebra,* or *iambic pentameter.* As you can see, there are degrees of "knownness" and "unknownness." Teaching about new concepts requires building on whatever knowledge base the student already has. Much content area vocabulary teaching is of label and concept unknown, meaning thoroughly new words.

All right. We have begged the issue long enough. We have reduced the need to teach vocabulary to the extent possible through the use of context and structural analysis. We have identified the words crucial to understanding. We have decided whether to teach for recognition or production. We have thought in terms of concept and label what the words might represent to our students. It is time to get on with it—time to teach vocabulary.

In order for vocabulary instruction to make sense to you and to your students, it must meet three essential criteria:

1. It must be efficient. As important, even crucial, as vocabulary is to the study of any subject, it is not the subject. There is simply not enough time in the teacher's day to give over a great deal of it to vocabulary instruction. In addition, teacher planning time is not abundant either. Thus, efficient instruction here means both efficient in terms of instruction and in terms of teacher planning time.

2. Effective vocabulary instruction must also proceed from the teacher's knowledge about what the words represent to the students in terms of label and concept.

3. Vocabulary instruction must also be purpose driven. Since time is limited and since acquisition is need-driven anyway, words and concepts central to the purpose for reading must be the ones selected for instruction.

VOCABULARY INSTRUCTION

Prereading Vocabulary Instruction

The best results are obtained when students are given the opportunity to see the words in meaningful sentences, hear them used in meaningful sentences, say the words themselves, and write the words in meaningful sentences. In addition, vocabulary instruction must be efficient in the ways described above. It must also be effective and get the job done. The following basic lesson plan meets all of these criteria.

Elements of the Basic Prereading Vocabulary Lesson Plan

1. The students encounter the word in the actual context in which they will read it or, if it is not possible for some reason to use the real context, in a rich context.

2. The teacher reads the sentence.

3. The class discusses the word and agrees on a definition. The teacher leads and shapes this discussion, but does not provide a definition. In this way, definitions in the students' own language are more likely. For example,

the students who defined *geology* as "the study of rock, no roll" created a perfectly serviceable definition *for their need.* If the students cannot produce a usable definition, the teacher has two options: (1) the teacher can provide a definition or (2) a previously appointed oracle (or sage, or savant), equipped with a good dictionary and adept at using it, can search for one while the class moves on to the next word. If the definition comes from the teacher or dictionary, the students should reword it in their own language.

4. The students write (in notebooks, on vocabulary cards, whatever) the teacher-shaped, class-generated definition.

5. The teacher asks the students to create new sentences using the word. The teacher and the class together decide on one or two of the best sentences and those are put on the board or overhead for the students to copy into their notebooks.

This simple five-step plan allows the students to hear the word in a real context, see the word in a real context, listen to and participate in a discussion wherein the word is defined in terms meaningful to them, write the word and its definition, hear and/or create other real contexts for the word, and write the word in more than one meaningful context. The method is quick, taking from ninety seconds to two minutes per word when students are familiar with the technique.

Notice that this technique is done before students read a chapter or a passage. Prereading vocabulary work like this gives students a preview of the main ideas (via the carefully selected vocabulary) and helps them with difficult words and concepts before they read. Prereading vocabulary instruction gives students more to bring to the reading—more experience and a higher sense of purpose.

Once the words have been introduced, discussed, and defined in this way, proceed on the assumption that the words are now a part of the students' working vocabulary (recognition or production) and act accordingly. That is, use the words in class discussions and on tests and quizzes just as any other words would be used.

Postreading Vocabulary Review Activities

At the beginning of the previous chapter it was suggested that knowing the vocabulary of a discipline represents a big step toward knowing the discipline. It follows, then, that a good vocabulary review is, or can be, a good review of the material and the concepts studied. *Review,* by

definition, means "after reading." Postreading vocabulary work extends students' knowledge of central ideas.

The review activities listed below can properly be thought of as a chapter or section review *through* vocabulary. If your goal is production of vocabulary, review is especially useful.

1. Prepare a handout with the words in sentences, leaving blank lines for the definition to be written in and blank lines for a sentence to be written in.
   a. Use for a small-group discussion activity. You might include points for each definition, for the best definition, or for the best sentence using the words.
   b. Use for a whole-class activity with variations as above in (a).

2. Prepare a handout with the target words deleted from their contexts and grouped at the bottom of the page. The task is for the students to place the words in their proper positions. (The words placed in the blanks should be written in, not simply indicated by number. Note also that this is a recognition activity unless the words are not listed on the page.)
   a. Use for a small-group activity as in #1 above.
   b. Use for a whole-class activity as in #1 above. It would be good to provide a space for original sentences, particularly if your goal is for production.

3. Prepare a handout with the review words and their definitions listed separately. The task is to match definition to word. Once again, the words should be written into the blanks, not indicated by number or lines or some such thing. This might be an individual or a small-group activity. (As described, this is a recognition activity, but, by deleting the word list, it can be made into a production activity.)

4. Have students work in groups to select key words from a chapter or unit and prepare a handout for other students to use, as in #1, #2, or #3 above. This can be effective when studying for an exam or quiz.

5. Use a separate 3 × 5 card for each word, its definition, and an appropriate sentence in card-sort activities.
   a. Mix the cards and have students match the words with sentences and definitions, or the words to sentences, or the words to definitions.
   b. Have students categorize the cards by the attributes of the words. When the vocabulary words represent concepts with relationships between them, this is an excellent activity for manipulating relationships. This production activity deepens students' knowledge of the words and their interrelatedness.

Reinforcement of Vocabulary Instruction

Vocabulary growth is a fairly slow process. It does not happen overnight. It is not reasonable to expect this skill to occur one Tuesday in October. We have argued that teaching the necessary vocabulary of a discipline is simply a part of teaching the discipline. You do not expect that instruction to be a one-shot, now-and-again proposition, and neither should you expect the attendant vocabulary instruction to be. It should be a long-term commitment. As such, it will need periodic review, as noted above, and reinforcement. Here are some techniques for reinforcement.

General Vocabulary Reinforcement Activities

1. Make it clear that when a word is introduced in class it is expected that the students will know it from then on. Students will find this reasonable as long as you carefully select the most crucial vocabulary to introduce.

2. Keep the words in view. This can be done with bulletin boards, posters, file boxes, notebooks, or on the chalkboard.

3. Use the words yourself. Try to use them in class discussions, in conversations with students, and, of course, on quizzes and tests.

4. Demonstrate that the words have an outside school reality. Ask students to find examples of the word's use in magazines and books, and in the speech of friends, parents, or television (see, for example, McKeown, Beck, Omanson, and Perfetti, 1983).

5. Make other teachers aware of the words you are teaching so they can, as the occasion permits, use the words in their classes. This can be done by posting the words in the teachers' lounge.

Specific In-Class Vocabulary Reinforcement Activities

1. Have students create crossword puzzles for other students to do. (This allows students to write the word and think about its definition.)

2. Have students create their own additional sentences using the words. Create a special bulletin board to post the most original, clever, outrageous—or whatever—sentence. (This allows students to use the word in their own language.)

3. Have whole-class review sessions with teams of students wherein a team can win points by:
   a. Giving a good definition of a word supplied by the teacher
   b. Saying the right word in response to a definition supplied by the teacher
   c. Using the word correctly in a sentence.
   (These activities allow the students to hear the words, definitions, and meaningful sentences using the words.

4. Keep a loose-leaf notebook of all words introduced. Shift the responsibility for maintaining this notebook from student to student. This becomes the classroom dictionary and, thereby, a ready reference for students and teacher.

EVALUATION OF VOCABULARY INSTRUCTION

It has been argued throughout this and the previous chapter that vocabulary instruction is an integral part of teaching whatever subject you teach. It is not a separate issue. For that reason, if for no other, we will argue that vocabulary should not be evaluated separately. In short, no vocabulary quizzes. Further, we have suggested that you decide whether you are teaching for recognition or production of vocabulary. Evaluation must be on the same basis. It would be extremely unfair to teach for recognition but test for production. On the other hand, teaching for production but testing only for recognition would not give you much of a measure of the success of the teaching or learning. So, two decisions must be made in evaluating vocabulary instruction: *how* and *when* to evaluate.

How to evaluate is easy. If you have chosen your vocabulary words wisely and well, they will be words crucial to the unit of study. Your evaluation will consist of how well your students use the words in responding to test questions (production) or how well your students understand the words in order to respond to test questions (recognition).

When to evaluate vocabulary instruction is within your other evaluation, such as chapter or unit tests or quizzes.

For production, note which questions logically call for terms you have taught and build into the points for those questions some value for the correct use of vocabulary. You can do this simply by including in the directions a notation that "The point value for this questions includes X points for vocabulary."

For recognition, just use the words as needed in writing the questions.

CLOSING STATEMENT

Words are properly thought of as labels for concepts. To say a person thoroughly understands a word is, really, to say that she or he understands the concept the word labels. Thus, when we talk about learning words, we mean it in the sense of learning the concepts labeled by the words. Words "learned" without that depth are just noises in the stream of speech or squiggles on a page.

REFERENCES

BECK, ISABEL L., AND MCKEOWN, MARGARET G. "Teaching Vocabulary: Making the Instruction Fit the Goal," *Educational Perspectives*, 23, 1985, 11–15.

GRAVES, MICHAEL F. "The Roles of Instruction in Fostering Vocabulary Development." In Margaret G. McKeown and Mary E. Curtis (Eds.), *The Nature of Vocabulary Acquisition*. Hillsdale, NJ: Lawrence Erlbaum, 1987, pp. 165–184.

JENKINS, JOSEPH R., AND DIXON, ROBERT. "Vocabulary Learning," *Contemporary Educational Psychology*, 8, 1983, 237–260.

MCKEOWN, MARGARET G.; BECK, ISABEL L.; OMANSON, RICHARD C.; AND PERFETTI, CHARLES A. "The Effects of Long-Term Vocabulary Instruction on Reading Comprehension: A Replication," *Journal of Reading Behavior*, 15, 1983, 3–18.

STERNBERG, ROBERT J. "Most Vocabulary Is Learned from Context." In Margaret G. McKeown and Mary E. Curtis (Eds.), *The Nature of Vocabulary Acquisition*. Hillsdale, NJ: Lawrence Erlbaum, 1987, pp. 89–105.

6

COMPREHENSION: QUESTIONS FOR UNDERSTANDING

Your Old Man took her diamonds
And tiaras by the score
Now she gets her kicks in Stepney
Not in Knightsbridge anymore*

Do you understand the above? Sure, you say. Cover the lyrics and answer these questions: What jewelry items are mentioned? Who "took" these items? Not difficult, right? Now refer to the passage and try these: In what sense is the word *took* being used here—to bring to or to steal from? What is the relationship between the person being addressed and "your Old Man"? Who is "her"? Compare and contrast Stepney and Knightsbridge. It's a little more difficult, isn't it? Now try these: Why have the authors chosen direct address (first person) rather than indirect address (second person)? How do you respond to people who own (or have owned) "diamonds and tiaras by the score"? If this passage refers to someone who has suffered an economic loss, what is your response to that? Sorrow? Secret glee? Indifference? Why do you feel that way?

Do you think your ability to answer these questions would be

*Nanker Phelge "Play with Fire," ABKCO Music, Inc. Used with permission.

enhanced if we provided you a reason for reading the passage and thinking carefully about it? Do you think your ability to answer the questions would be further enhanced if we gave you some appropriate background information? The answers to both questions must, of course, be yes. That is what this chapter is about: levels of understanding and the questions that you can select to achieve those levels, and the ways in which purpose setting and background building (what we referred to as *bridge building* in Chapter 1) can help you nudge your students to higher levels of understanding.

The levels of understanding we will discuss are represented in the series of questions posed above about the Rolling Stones' song lyric. The first set of questions is *literal*. The second set is *inferential*. The third set is what we will call *higher-than-inferential*. We will discuss these terms later.

READING COMPREHENSION AND LEVELS OF UNDERSTANDING

How do people understand what they read? What occurs within an individual's mind that allows him or her to comprehend? How can teachers know when students understand? More to the point, how can comprehension be increased? People interested in the phenomenon of reading have argued these questions for years. Although the answers have varied from expert to expert and era to era, some things are known and some answers can be given.

Briefly, reading comprehension appears to depend very heavily on vocabulary, as we noted earlier. In several classic research studies vocabulary strength was shown to be the most powerful component of reading comprehension. (For an excellent overview of this research, see Anderson and Freebody, 1981, or, for a more extensive and varied look, see McKeown and Curtis, 1987.) The stronger the vocabulary, the better the reading comprehension. That, in part, is why this book has two chapters on vocabulary instruction.

In addition to vocabulary strength, what people already know influences what they can learn from reading. Relevant previous experience, whether direct or vicarious (from reading, television, movies, etc.), plays an important role in reading comprehension. (See the discussion of our definition of reading in Chapter 1.) Consider this:

Slowly people accustomed themselves to the idea that the physical states of space itself were the final physical reality.

The above quotation, which contains no terribly difficult words and no horribly convoluted syntax, is probably pretty near meaningless to most people. Most individuals have no experience, real or vicarious, to which they can relate the quotation. If we fill in your experience a bit by telling you that the quotation is from Albert Einstein, that might help. If we were to write a little background piece on Einstein's ideas and his importance to the world of science in general and to the world of physics in particular, that would help. If, in addition to all of that, we were meeting face to face and we could contrive clever ways to help you bring your personal experience to bear in understanding the quotation, that would help greatly. If we could then give you a good clear purpose for understanding, then—and probably only then—could you really read and profit from reading the quotation.

Thus, in a very real way, reading comprehension takes place both before and after reading. The *before* part includes what Pearson and Johnson (1978) have called building "the bridge between the new and the known." Much of this bridge is built through careful and thoughtful purpose setting. You, as the teacher, are the chief architect of that bridge between what your students already know and what you want them to learn. The *after* part might be thought of as bridge checking, repairing, and shoring up as needed. Questions are useful in both parts.

PURPOSE SETTING

What do you want your students to get from what you ask them to read? That is text purpose setting and it is very important. How many times has an instructor simply told you to "read Chapter Nine"? Were you supposed to study it closely for a lot of detailed information? To relate it to some previously read chapter? To read it for broad background information? If the instructor did not set a purpose or help you set one for yourself, you had no way of knowing. Were you ever skunked on a quiz or a test because you had done the required reading for broad background information and you found, after the fact, that the instructor wanted detailed information?

Clear purpose setting means that the material to be read is introduced to the students in such a way that the following questions are answered: (1) From the title of this section (or chapter or unit), what should my students expect to gain from this reading? This kind of focus question helps give students an investment in what they read. (Now, textbooks titles tend to be pretty explicit. However, titles for supplementary readings from trade books or magazines may not be. Where the title *doesn't* provide much information, you can skip this question.) (2) What do my students already know about this topic? Since knowledge builds on knowledge, this is tacit recognition of the importance of prior knowledge to the learning task at hand. That knowledge, by the way, comes from a variety of sources, not the least of which is prior schooling. Some of that "knowledge," however, will actually be misconception. This is the place to deal with that. (3) Where does this fit into what we have been studying? This is a natural place for a quick review that ties the present task into previous work. In introducing the text and setting the expectations, the teacher should make certain that the answers to these questions, not the questions themselves, are clear to the students. The example below will serve to illustrate.

Let us assume a tenth-grade American history class is about to read a chapter entitled "The American Civil War: Origins of the Conflict." The preceding chapter compared the political, social, and economic systems of the North and South. The following two chapters detail the first and second halves of the Civil War. Let us further assume that the teacher is attempting to show how this particular event in American history has parallels in past and present internecine conflicts. With this overview in mind, consider the previously asked questions one at a time.

From the title of this chapter, what should my students expect to gain from this reading?

Obviously, the chapter title, "The American Civil War: Origins of the Conflict," tells quite a lot. However, it does not tell all, nor should it. In this case, the teacher wishes to dispel the rather common assumption that slavery was the only issue in the war. Thus, the teacher guides the discussion of the chapter title and what it might presage by emphasizing that the key word, *origins*, is plural. The students, then, should expect to gain some understanding of the multiple causes of the conflict.

What do my students already know about this topic?

The answer is a lot. They have learned in the preceding chapter about some crucial differences between the North and the South. The teacher does a quick review of that chapter, eliciting students' predictions about how the differences they already know about might have brought the two societies into conflict. In addition, as just noted, the teacher wants to be certain to dispel the preconception that the war had a single cause.

Where does this fit into what we have been studying?

In this example, this question is already pretty much answered by drawing upon students' knowledge of war gained from the previous chapter. However, it is worth noting that the teacher's goal is, in part, to draw parallels between the American Civil War and other civil wars of past and present. This is the logical place to do that.

The important points in all of this are that the teacher has the responsibility of establishing purpose and conveying that purpose to students in an understandable, meaningful way. There is no reason for secrecy. Students then know what is expected from them, and the teacher has a legitimate base from which to guide discussions, make additional assignments, and evaluate student learning.

Clear and careful purpose setting is neither difficult nor time consuming. It is just good teaching.

QUESTIONING

Having set your students off on the proper reading course through careful purpose setting, how do you find out whether they have gotten there — that is, whether they have successfully understood the material? Simple. Ask them. Well, it's not really that simple. You have to know what to ask them. It will help if you select questions related to your purpose for assigning the material and choose from the range of question types discussed next.

A Simplified Taxonomy of Questions

The range of questions discussed below is not intended to serve as a psychological model of comprehension or even as an exhaustive review of question types. Rather, it is intended to serve as a guide to the broad range of questions that you can ask, to suggest some ways for you to respond to students' answers, and to relate discussion questions to reading/listening purpose. The taxonomy has three levels — literal, inferential, and higher-than-inferential.

Literal Level. Literal level questions are *text-bound*. They ask for an answer that is stated directly in the text.

Obviously, even at this fairly low level, literal-level questions have a broad range of difficulty and worth. For example, in a story about a boy going to the store to buy milk, bread, and eggs and carrying those items home in his yellow wagon, what he bought, what he carried it home in, and his sex are only important literal-level items relative to whatever else happens in the story. If, as the story unfolds, there is a search for a boy and his red wagon, then the color of our hero's wagon becomes important. If, however, the story unfolds in the direction of what use was made of the grocery items, then the color of the wagon is not as important. All that suggests is that literal-level questions be chosen on the basis of their importance to the entire story and their importance to the purpose for which the story was read. Unfortunately, many literal-level questions that are essentially irrelevant are posed in classes every day.

Now, if the material being read is not a simple fictional account (narrative) but is, instead, a relatively complex and sophisticated discussion of cell division (expository), the same principles hold true. Importance is relative. Facts are important in relation to the total piece and to the reason and the purpose for reading it.

Responses to literal-level questions are either right or wrong. Handling correct responses is easy. An enthusiastic "yes" or "very good" is all that is needed. Handling a wrong response is a bit more difficult. You don't want to discourage the student from trying, yet, at the same time, you must not accept a wrong answer. A good way to handle a wrong response is to simply say "no" or "that's not it" and give some positive reinforcement for the effort.

Inferential Level. Inferential questions are *text plus* questions. The plus is the ability of the reader/listener to put together facts (literal) in order to infer from them something not directly stated in the text. For example, adding to the previous example the time of day the boy went to buy the groceries, it might be logical to infer that he was buying breakfast essentials. This might be an inference worth making if it is important as the story unfolds. If it is not, it still represents good inferential reasoning but reasoning which, at least in this case, is not essential to understanding the story.

Again, if the material is expository, not narrative, as in the example, the principles remain true except that appropriate inferences are likely to be more narrowly circumscribed. For example, a reading selection on cell division is unlikely to lend itself to a great number of inferences since it is likely such things as sequence and cause and effect—the usual stuff of which inferences are made—are clearly stated. If they are not, they are logical sources for the type of inferential questions such as "What must come first?" or "What causes this?"

Inferences can be relatively low level, even trivial. For example, if we now refer to them as "them" (as we have just done), you, the reader, must infer that "them" refers to "inferences." This is pretty low-level stuff that most people are not bothered by in the least. Still, that single word ("them") now has come to stand for the whole business of inference and inference skills—not a simple subject. At the other end of the scale, Flood (1981) offers the example "It was a typical January day in Stockholm." Note what a burden of inference the author has put on the reader in terms of his or her prior experience. Beyond assuming that it would be cold, we have no idea what a typical January day in Stockholm would be like. Would it be dark and stormy or bright and calm? Would the days be terribly short and the nights dreadfully long?

Responses to inferential questions are more likely to be on-target or off-target than they are to be clearly right or wrong. Good inferential questions almost always require a tag question such as "Why do you think that?" or, simply, "Why?" The strength of an answer to an inferential question lies in the facts that can be marshalled to support it, providing an excellent reason for students to refer back to and reread parts of the text. However, according to a report derived from the National Assessment of Educational Progress (Petrosky, 1982), one of the weakest areas of secondary school students' performance is in the area of defending and explaining the inferences they make. Still, where an answer is fact-based, it most likely will not be dead wrong. It can be weak, it can be off-target, it can represent lousy reasoning, but it probably won't be totally wrong. Therefore, such responses should not be labeled incorrect. They should be accepted as "point of view" or an "interesting way of looking at it," or simply recognized for how close to the target they came.

Higher-Than-Inferential Level. H-T-I questions are *text plus plus* questions. The first plus is for inferential; the second one involves the reader's/listener's individual experience, feelings, and thinking about the story or text. As with the other categories, some H-T-I questions are better than others. The classic H-T-I question for application, and one that students come to loathe, is "What did you learn from this story?" (And, over the course of several years of such questions, what they've learned is that they better come up with some answer to the question "What did you learn from this story?") A better use for this level of involvement in a story or any text is one that allows the readers/listeners to unite their own feelings, experiences, and thoughts with those of the characters in the story or to try to imagine what the information gained from expository material may mean to them personally. For example, asking the students whether they've had experiences or feelings similar to those described in the story or asking if they would have behaved the same or differently under the story's circumstances, allows them to think about the material from their own unique and individual perspectives.

The H-T-I level represents an opportunity that is too little used with expository reading. For example, in the expository piece on cell division, the relevance of normal cell division to a host of health concerns might be established by discussion and careful questioning. (As near as we are able to determine, malignant [cancer] cells multiply in the same way as benign normal cells. Therefore, the fight against cancer is greatly aided by all the acquired information on cell division.)

As with inferential questions, but perhaps to a greater degree, H-T-I responses, again when they are clearly based on the material, usually are not simply right or wrong. Since H-T-I questions elicit experience and feeling, it is extremely important that the responses be treated with a great deal of respect. Sometimes, by way of an example, students will seem unduly harsh in their judgments of a person's actions. They will be quick to label a political, historical, or literary figure as a fool or coward. No matter how harsh or, from your point of view, unfair the judgments are, it is the students' right to feel that way and to respond that way. No one's response to an H-T-I question should be belittled. Responses can be explained further, expanded upon, always brought back to the text, but they can't be put down.

Using All Three Levels

What is a reasonable mix of questions for a discussion? That depends on what you want from the discussion—purpose, again. If you want to get at the theme of a piece, then designing literal and inferential questions that elicit the information necessary to recognize the theme is all that is required. Enough is enough. If what you want is a broad exploration of student reaction to and knowledge of the piece, then a variety of questions at the literal and inferential levels is necessary, and although you will have planned H-T-I questions according to the purpose, you will probably have to come up with some others as you go. The reason for this is that you must pick up on students' reactions and you can't predict those in advance. So, you see, the questions and the mix of questions cannot be separated from the goals of the discussion which, of course, grow out of the stated purpose for reading. Think carefully about what you want and design your questions accordingly. We give two examples of question planning later in this chapter, and in Chapter 7 we suggest several methods for structuring discussions.

Some disciplines are more fact-laden than others. We can easily imagine the response of some science and math teachers while reading about levels of questions. They are saying, sure, all that is fine, but how do I ask higher-order questions about quadratic equations? Or how do I ask higher-order questions about eutrophication? Well, you've got us. We have only the haziest notion of eutrophication and not the slightest idea of quadratic equations and what one does with them. And that's the point. Science and mathematics affect our lives in thousands of ways of which most of us are completely unaware. If you are a scientist or mathematician, your respective discipline is a wondrously interesting complex of facts and theories and suppositions from facts and theories. If able scientists, for example, did not *infer* relationships between and among facts, all they would have is a collection of disordered and unrelated facts. If able mathematicians did not make judgments about how mathematics facts could be applied (remember, application is higher-than-inferential), all they would have is endless, unrelated, and unordered formulas. The point being made here is that although science and mathematics may be more fact-laden, they are still disciplines that lend themselves to higher-order questions. Remember the bridge between the new and the known? It is just as important in science and math as it is in any other field. In fact, it may be more important because we suspect that that particular bridge is less traveled and most in need of repair.

Two Examples of Purposeful Questioning

The two examples that follow use the same short piece, entitled "The Mission," but for two different classes and for two different purposes.

The Mission

An old man and a young boy were walking along the deserted street that ran next to the railroad tracks. That part of town was largely inhabited by dilapidated, greying buildings that had once served as warehouses for goods destined for booming Alaska. The old man was dressed in an outdated, somewhat worn but very clean dark blue pin-striped suit. It was the kind of suit one might have seen on a prosperous banker thirty years ago. The old man walked steadily, though not swiftly, on legs that apparently pained him at the knees. The boy was wearing new dark blue pants, a new white shirt, a light blue jacket, new and somewhat dusty black shoes, and no cap. The boy's clothes, though new, were obviously of poor quality and would soon look shabby.

The boy would run ahead of the old man and then be distracted by a broken bottle or a piece of twisted metal, stop to examine it and, in the process, fall behind the old man. However often that happened, the boy never let the old man get more than twenty feet ahead of him. And he never ventured more than twenty feet ahead of the old man.

They didn't speak. Perhaps they didn't have to.

CLASS: *EIGHTH-GRADE LANGUAGE ARTS*

Unit: Descriptive writing

Reading purpose: Read to see how the author uses details (1) to create a picture, (2) to compare and contrast people to place, and (3) to hint at what may be a very complex relationship.

Vocabulary: dilapidated

Questions to guide discussion: (Note: Not to be followed slavishly. Not all listed questions *need* be asked, and many not listed *may* be asked. Think of these questions as the framework of the discussion. Note that they are keyed to the purpose stated.)

Literal:

1. What is the condition of the old man's clothing? The boy's?

2. What is the state of the area through which they are walking?

3. How is the old man's walk described?

4. How far away from the old man does the boy venture?

Inferential:

1. Are these two people related in some way? Why do you think that?

2. Are these two people out of place in their present surroundings? Why do you think that?

3. Why is it that the boy doesn't ever get very far from the old man? What makes you think that?

4. Why don't the two characters talk to one another? Why do you think that?

Higher-Than-Inferential:

1. In what ways are the people and place contrasted and compared?

2. Is the author's rather sparing use of details effective in creating a picture of the people and place? Why or why not?

3. Would the description be better or worse if the two characters carried on a conversation? Why?

Description of the lesson: The teacher is using this piece as part of a unit on descriptive writing. Specifically, the teacher will ask the students to read to see how the author uses details to (1) create a picture, (2) compare and contrast people to place, and (3) hint at what may be a very complex relationship between the two people described.

From the title of the piece, the students may get very little. But they may come up with two rather different interpretations of the word *mission* — one having a sense similar to a quest and the other relating to missions that help to feed, clothe, and house the down and out and homeless.

What the students already know about this topic is twofold. The topic of descriptive writing is one they have been working on, and they have a developing good sense of it. The other, the piece itself, dealing as it does with the less fortunate, will call for the teacher to explore the students' responses to the plight of people like the ones described.

The reading purpose, as stated, tells the students directly how this fits into what they have been studying.

Now, consider the same piece as it might be used in an American History class on the Great Depression. Notice how the different purpose changes the questions. What were appropriate questions for the descriptive writing purpose become, for the most part, inappropriate for the history purpose.

CLASS: ELEVENTH-GRADE SOCIAL STUDIES, AMERICAN HISTORY

Topic: Introduction to pre-World War II American History: The Great Depression

Supplementary reading: "The Mission."

Reading purpose: Here is a glimpse of what the Great Depression wrought in human terms. Read to note the sense of loss and despair conveyed by this piece, but note also that there is a sense of hope undimmed.

Vocabulary: none

Questions to guide discussion: (Again, not to be followed slavishly. These questions represent the framework of the discussion. Note that these questions are keyed to this purpose and although some are similar, they would not, as a group, be appropriate for the Language Arts purpose.)

Literal:

1. What is the condition of the area in which the pair walks?

2. What is the condition of the man's clothing? The boy's?

3. Are there human voices heard in this scene?

Inferential:

1. In some past time, what was the condition of the area in which the pair walks? What makes you think that?

2. Of the man and the boy, who is taking care of whom? Why do you say that?

3. Are there any sounds heard in this scene?

Higher-Than-Inferential:

1. Where are the man and the boy going? Why do you say that?

2. What will become of the man and the boy? What makes you think that?

3. Why are there no sounds, human or otherwise, mentioned?

As suggested above, all of these questions are designed to convey to the students a sense of the human cost of the Great Depression.

Description of the lesson: From the title of this piece in the context of their study of the depression, the students might speculate that the title refers to a political or economic mission. They might also know about soup kitchens of the era and see the title as referring to that kind of mission. All would be useful in bridge-building terms.

What the students already know about the topic they may have gotten from grandparents, great grandparents, or classic movies such as *The Grapes of Wrath.* In any event, they will have some knowledge and, most likely, some misconceptions about the topic. The teacher will explore what is known and try to eliminate the misconceptions.

The teacher plans a quick review of post-World War I America and the Roaring Twenties to demonstrate how this topic relates to what went before.

CLOSING STATEMENT

Reading is not done for itself; it is done for a reason or purpose. That purpose is, broadly speaking, understanding. We have argued that it is the teacher's obligation to guide that understanding by teaching the vocabulary necessary, by bringing to conscious level what is already known about the topic, by stating good and clear purposes for reading, and by designing questions that probe and enhance that understanding. The next chapter offers some discussion techniques that build on the ideas presented here.

REFERENCES

ANDERSON, RICHARD C., AND FREEBODY, PETER. "Vocabulary Knowledge." In John T. Guthrie (Ed.), *Comprehension and Teaching: Research Reviews*. Newark, DE: International Reading Association, 1981, pp. 77–117.

FLOOD, JAMES. "Prose Comprehension: A Selected Review of Literature on Inference-Generation as a Requisite for Understanding Text." In D. F. Fisher and C. W. Peters (Eds.), *Comprehension and the Competent Reader: Interdisciplinary Perspectives*. New York: Praeger, 1981.

McKEOWN, MARGARET G., AND CURTIS, MARY E. (EDS.). *The Nature of Vocabulary Acquisition*. Hillsdale, NJ: Lawrence Erlbaum, 1987.

PEARSON, P. DAVID, AND JOHNSON, DALE. *Teaching Reading Comprehension*. New York: Holt, Rinehart & Winston, 1978.

PETROSKY, ANTHONY R. "Reading Achievement." In Allen Berger and H. Alan Robinson (Eds.), *Secondary School Reading: What Research Reveals for Classroom Practice*. Urbana, IL: National Council of Teachers of English, 1982, pp. 7–20.

7

COMPREHENSION: DISCUSSIONS FOR UNDERSTANDING

Have you ever sat in on a class discussion that deteriorated into a bull session? Of course you have. You may even have enjoyed it. Or perhaps you were extremely put off by it or by someone who dominated it and used it as a forum for his or her particular views. Whether you enjoyed it or not, you were probably fully aware that such discussions serve no real educational function. (They may serve a psychological function, but that is a different story.) Did you ever see panic in a teacher's eyes when she or he saw the discussion slipping away and seemed incapable of doing anything about it? Did you ever wonder how or why that happened?

Useful discussion of a topic in a whole class or small group, whether in advance of reading about it as a way of bridge building and purpose setting or after reading about it as a way of enhancing and informally or formally evaluating comprehension, does not magically occur. It takes careful and thoughtful preparation. A good deal of that thought and much of that preparation involves knowing how to conduct discussions and knowing what you, as the discussion leader, want from the discussion.

Just as you will surely have a variety of purposes for the reading assignments you make, so should you have a variety of techniques for using the reading. In the previous chapter we argued for and illustrated the importance of purpose setting and questioning at all levels. In this chapter

we build on those basic themes through an exploration of discussion strategies.

CONDUCTING DISCUSSIONS

The kind of discussion you plan for should be a mix of your purpose for the discussion and your own personal style—what you are comfortable with. Think of the possibilities as ranging from wide open to structured.

A wide open, free-wheeling discussion is useful for introducing large topics, exploring responses to some current event, or conducting a wide-ranging review. For example, a biology teacher we observed opened his class by asking the question "Why should we study biology?" In order to encourage broad and irreverent discussion, he put on the board as the first reason "To keep Mr. Williams employed." He encouraged both silly and serious responses and, as you might expect, got them. But because he knew where he wanted the discussion to go and because he kept the silliness within tolerable limits by verbal reinforcement of serious and thoughtful responses, he got a good and lively discussion. What purposes were served by this kind of discussion? Some very good ones, actually. Through the less serious responses, the students were able to talk about some of their fears and misconceptions about the subject. The teacher was able to be reassuring and to clear up some misconceptions. Through the more serious responses, the teacher was able to give a good overview of the subject and to connect it to the students' lives. Besides all that, the first biology class of that semester was fun for the students and, we suspect, the teacher as well. There is nothing like a good beginning unless, of course, it is a happy ending.

A more structured approach is one we refer to as a *topics-centered free discussion*. In such a discussion the students are assigned subtopics within the larger topic and speak from their own "expertise" during the discussion. For example, by way of introducing a unit on World War II to an American history class, a teacher assigned readings on various aspects of that era to small groups. One group took "The Mood on the Homefront," another took "The State of the Prewar Military," still another took "The Political Issues of the Time," and so on. These things then became the topics for a semi-structured discussion with the various groups speaking from their "specialties" and questioning the other groups about what they had found. This discussion was relatively unstructured within the structure provided by the various subtopics.

Again, what purposes were served by this kind of discussion? As noted, this was the introduction to a rather large unit on World War II. The teacher knew what general topics she wanted to follow throughout that unit, and she used those as the basis for the small-group work. So, what she got was a good introduction to the unit, good bridge building (connecting to what the students already knew), and good motivation to study the era. For such a discussion to be successful for all involved, it had to lead to greater overall understanding. (Nothing would be served by having groups of students knowledgeable only about some aspect of the topic.) So, the discussion ended with class-generated notes summarizing the discussion. Each group had to be satisfied that its information was adequately represented in the summary notes. This style of discussion can be done without the prereading by having students brainstorm in small groups about subtopics within a larger topic and conducting the discussion from there.

A much more focused prereading discussion style, one we aptly, yet plainly, refer to as *structured*, serves to explore the students' knowledge about some large topic before they read about it. If the biology teacher we referred to earlier wanted to accomplish similar goals in a first-day discussion about the study of his subject and if he were comfortable with a less free-wheeling approach, he might have chosen to conduct a structured discussion. To do so, he would have planned for the discussion by listing the points he wanted to make and writing questions at the various levels of understanding about these points. In class he would have either listed these points on the board or overhead and used his questions about each as his discussion guide. Or he could have given each general point to a small group to discuss; each group would prepare to speak to the larger group about the topic. These points, then, would have provided the structure and, assuming he wrote good questions, his purposes—to introduce the topic, to clear up any misconceptions about it, and to get a sense of the students' attitudes toward it—would have been served.

In these three discussion styles it is apparent that the teacher needs to have a clear purpose in mind and be able to lead and shape the discussion through the use of questions at all levels. In the next section, we explain several well-known discussion techniques that combine reading and discussion in prescribed and purpose-centered ways.

DISCUSSION TECHNIQUES

The Directed Reading-Thinking Activity, DR-TA (Stauffer and Cramer, 1969), and the Guided Reading Procedure, GRP (Manzo, 1975, 1985), are prereading strategies designed to enhance student engagement in reading through the use of predictions. Prediction and prediction strategies serve the content area teacher in two important ways. They engage the students in what they are reading and bring the students' prior experiences to bear upon the reading to be done.

Engagement here means giving the students a stake in what they are reading. For example, we might ask you to predict, based on your reading thus far and on your other relevant experiences, where this chapter is likely to take you. If we could sit with you, face to face, and get your predictions and prod you a bit to elaborate on them, you would have a stake in the reading in that your natural desire to find out whether or to what degree you were right would help to propel you through the material. Your students are no different. Prediction is an element of each of the strategies discussed below. Let us consider them one at a time.

The Directed Reading-Thinking Activity

The DR-TA is probably the best known of the formal prereading lesson plan strategies. Essentially, it is designed to move the student from the higher-than-inferential level of understanding through the inferential and to the literal and back again. This is accomplished by having the students make the broadest predictions possible about a piece based only on its title or a sentence or two of the text. The predictions are recorded (on blackboard or overhead), a short section of the piece is read, and the predictions are retained, modified, or discarded. Through this process of prediction and refinement of prediction, the students are brought into the text.

Steps in DR-TA

1. *Prediction.*   Using the title of the piece or, if a textbook, the chapter title and section headings, ask: "What do you think this will be about?" In order to encourage the broadest possible speculation, accept and record all reasonable responses. For each response recorded, ask: "Why do you think so?" As we noted in Chapter 6, asking students to predict from a title enables you to set the direction for reading and clear up misunderstandings.

2. *Refining and extending.*   Assign a short portion of the text to students to read silently, or read the portion yourself. The length of passage will vary considerably with the purpose for the reading and the length of the piece. As a general rule, we have found that 300- to 500-word sections, one to three minutes of reading time, work best. For younger students or for more difficult material, you may have to use shorter sections. You will have to experiment a bit to find what is best for your group. When all have finished, go back through the predictions already recorded and ask, for each one: "Do we retain, modify, or discard this one? Why?" Then ask for any new predictions and, of course, why the person responding thinks that.

3. *Conclusion.*   Repeat steps #1 and #2 for the portion of the material you have decided on. Probably three to five sections is optimal. If the entire piece has been read, move to your postreading plan. If the entire piece has not been read, plan so that the students are given time to finish the reading.

It should be evident that the DR-TA moves from the broad to the specific and that it is an excellent way to get students into the material. Your purpose for the reading will, of course, dictate your postreading plan.

The Guided Reading Procedure

The Guided Reading Procedure, GRP, is the conceptual opposite of the DR-TA in that it builds from the specific to the broad. Its best use is to emphasize the importance of literal understanding as the foundation for inferential and higher-than-inferential understanding. Because GRP is so highly structured, we follow Manzo (1975) in recommending that it be used infrequently, no more than once a week, and further suggest that its best use is as an introduction to fairly heavy fact-laden material. After setting the purpose for reading, as described in the previous chapter, follow these steps.

Steps in GRP

1. Select a portion of text to be read. For most purposes, 800 to 1000 words, roughly four to seven minutes, is a good length.

2. In addition to the purpose setting already done, ask the students to retain as many *details* as possible.

3. When students have finished the reading, they place the material face down on their desks. Then ask the students to recall as much as possible, recording their recollections on the board or overhead. Prompt and probe with statements such as, "Is that all?" or "Anymore?" or "Can anyone add to this?"

4. At this point, review what is recorded, suggest that the information is incomplete (as it will be), and ask students to review the material read to locate any missing information.

5. When the review is complete, record the additional information.

6. Review all the information recorded and then organize it in some fashion. We have found this is the crucial step, because it is here that the teacher is able to move beyond the literal level.

7. Give students a short quiz—multiple choice, fill in the blank, or very short-answer essay. This step is crucial for two reasons. First and foremost, you want the students to have concrete evidence of their success at mastering the GRP piece. Consequently, the test should be relatively easy. Second,

you need some evaluation and some means of reinforcement of learning, both of which the test gives.

8. Students read the remainder of the text in the usual way.

The GRP emphasizes the importance of a literal base of understanding, but it does not stop there. It is, after all, a prereading strategy. Your postreading strategy, dictated by your purpose for reading, should move the students beyond the literal level.

ReQuest

ReQuest, short for reciprocal questioning (Manzo, 1969, 1985), is typically thought of as a comprehension instruction technique that is particularly useful for getting students beyond the literal level of comprehension. It accomplishes this by having the teacher model higher-order questions for the students (the questioning) and having the teacher praise and reinforce higher-order questions from students (the reciprocal questioning). As such, it can also be an excellent group study method.

Because it is done using small sections of text and because it is a fairly intense process, we have found ReQuest most useful with small groups (four to six students) as an introduction to the whole business of higher-order questioning (for which it was originally designed) or as a lead-in to concept-dense material. As with the DR-TA, prior vocabulary instruction and bridge building are prerequisites.

Steps in ReQuest

1. Teacher and students read a very small segment of text silently, as little as a single sentence but usually two or three sentences.

2. The students question the teacher, who has closed his or her book. The teacher answers literal questions without comment, and answers higher-order questions then rewards the question with praise.

3. Reverse roles. This time the students close their books and the teacher is the questioner. The teacher should pose good higher-order questions.

4. Proceed in this way, with exchanges of roles, using slightly larger text segments each time until enough material has been read to shift to the DR-TA style of prediction questions (i.e., "What do you think the rest of this is going to be about?" and "Why do you think so?").

5. The students finish reading the assignment.

Note: When students are first cast into the role of questioner of the teacher, you may find that they want to play stump the teacher. That is natural. If you are asked a question you can't answer, admit it. But if you discover that picayune literal questions are all you are getting, the process has broken down and the students need to be reminded that that is not the point.

CLOSING STATEMENT

We want to accomplish several things at once by conducting good discussions prompted and guided by questions carefully thought out in advance. First, we want to assess comprehension. That is, we want to see whether the purpose for reading was served. Second, a good discussion prods further comprehension. If you like to go to movies, it is likely that you do not go alone. When you see a movie with friends and then discuss it, your

perceptions of it and your understanding of it are probably influenced by the other persons' and theirs by yours. Their reactions to characters and events may be different from your own. They may know more or less than you about such technical matters as lighting and camera angles. They may get a joke or reference you didn't get. By discussing it, you all end up with more. The same is true for your students—by discussing a reading assignment, they end up with more.

REFERENCES

MANZO, ANTHONY V. "The ReQuest Procedure," *Journal of Reading, 13,* 1969, 123–126.

MANZO, ANTHONY V. "Guided Reading Procedure," *Journal of Reading, 18,* 1975, 287–291.

MANZO, ANTHONY V. "Expansion Modules for the ReQuest, CAT, GRP, and REAP Reading/Study Procedures," *Journal of Reading, 28,* 1985, 498–502.

STAUFFER, RUSSELL G., AND CRAMER, RONALD. *Teaching Critical Reading at the Primary Level.* Newark, DE: International Reading Association, 1969.

8

WRITING TO LEARN: REFLECTION ON LEARNING

Content area teachers are excited about writing. Excited? About carting home 150 five-paragraph essays with misspellings and sentence fragments? No, secondary teachers do not find joy in reading five-paragraph essays. They are learning instead the value of writing-to-learn, which decreases their reading time even though students write more, opens channels of communication between them and students, and engages their students in their content area.

Writing-to-learn does not mean "writing across the curriculum." Teachers "across the curriculum" balk because they know the real goal is to teach *writing*. This is not so with writing-to-learn—a tool to encourage student *thinking* about your content area, be it music, biology, art, or history. Because the writing is a means, not an end, the content area teacher worries less about the writing than about the student's thought and reflection.

Consider one use of writing to learn: two team teachers assign journals in integrated physics, mathematics, and computer programming classes to allow their students to reflect on what they learned, how they understood, and what they didn't understand. At times the students describe in words a concept or process they have learned. At other times, students confide confusion or fears or successes about the subject, as in these examples:

We did this weird thing on statistics. It seemed so stupid to me. I don't understand why we're doing this. I felt like a third grader.

Now I'm finding that I'm having another problem. I am forgetting what I understood at the very beginning.

I'm doing fine.

I didn't know that others in the class didn't understand. I thought it was just me.

The experiment in physics today helped me understand resistance.

Because the teachers' goals are students' reflections, not writing or spelling, they do not circle errors or place letter grades on the writing. Instead, they skim the journals and reinforce the students' reflection with a few words:

I think you have done a good analysis of the situation.

I appreciate the effort that goes into such thoughtful entries.

Let me know at the end of the week how you are feeling about statistics.

Thank you for being so clear about what seems to help you learn and what doesn't.

I enjoyed reading your journal.

The use of reflective or personal writing, as in journals, is the topic of this chapter. The next chapter describes more public and formal writing, such as themes and essays.

REFLECTIVE WRITING

Reflective writing increases communication between you and your students, allowing you access to their thought processes, as in the comments from the journals we just discussed. This writing is purposeful, connecting the topic of the class with the student's background experience in a purposeful way. Reflective writing provides a format for a student to recognize and deal with confusion and for you to know whether the student understands. Although teachers use various techniques to incorporate reflective writing in classes, the journal is the most popular. Teachers use journal writing successfully in mathematics, history, art, foreign languages, physics, English, social studies, and other content areas. Part of its allure comes from its flexibility.

THE JOURNAL

A journal is a student's think book for writing about a particular class; it is a daily notepad for ideas. Students usually buy a notebook specially for their journal, fostering involvement and ownership. Many teachers report that students keep their journals after the school year ends.

Recently, several student teachers told us about the remarkable changes that journal writing created in their classrooms. Late in the spring, battling spring fever and their own inexperience, these student teachers began assigning journal writing at the beginning of each class, providing topics about the lessons they were covering. Student interest rose and classroom discussions enlivened. "For the first time I really felt like I am going to be a teacher," one student teacher confided.

Experienced teachers appreciate the enthusiasm created by journals, but they also know that journal writing does not always produce instant results. For some students, the idea of reflecting about how they learn is so foreign that they are confused, asking, "What am I supposed to do?" Journal writing is far removed from filling-in-the-blanks or writing the standard five-paragraph essay. Not all students can write, without practice, about how they learned something or about problems they had in learning from a particular lesson. You can help by being patient and by modeling what you mean by reflective journal writing. Modeling occurs by sharing your own journal writings, by asking permission to read aloud perceptive entries, and by positively commenting on parts of a student's journal that are on track.

The use of journals originated in English classes to encourage fluency and confidence with writing and to help students generate writing topics (see Figure 8–1). For teachers of writing, the original use of journals remains helpful. But content area teachers value journals to encourage reflective thinking about the subject and about problems or successes the student has in learning. Your goal is writing-to-learn rather than learning-to-write.

Journal writing promotes key ideas in writing-to-learn: learner control, student responsibility, and student engagement with learning. This engagement is on an activity level, a mental level, and an emotional level, and, best of all, the journal encourages the involvement of the very bright and the weaker students. As one teacher of history for special education students notes, journals encourage "insights on an emotional involvement in learning. Students cannot sit through entire semesters with minimal engagement in the academic processes as some have routinely done for years" (Marik, 1985, p. 89). Students' emotional involvement with the content is one of the chief enticements of journal writing for many teachers. Journal writing offers one way of improving a student's relationship with the subject you teach.

Because journals are so flexible, you have options about classroom management of journals—whether to guide the topics or leave them open, whether to write in or out of class, when and how long to use them during the school year, how to collect and review the journals, and so on. We discuss all of these in the following sections of this chapter.

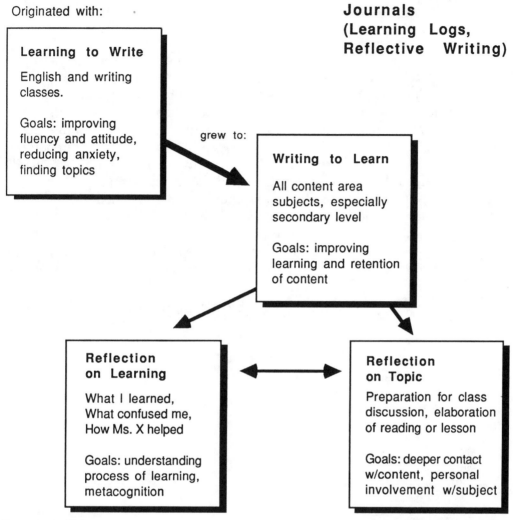

Originated with:

**Journals
(Learning Logs,
Reflective Writing)**

Learning to Write

English and writing classes.

Goals: improving fluency and attitude, reducing anxiety, finding topics

grew to:

Writing to Learn

All content area subjects, especially secondary level

Goals: improving learning and retention of content

Reflection on Learning

What I learned, What confused me, How Ms. X helped

Goals: understanding process of learning, metacognition

Reflection on Topic

Preparation for class discussion, elaboration of reading or lesson

Goals: deeper contact w/content, personal involvement w/subject

Commonalities
Teachers report good student attitude and interest.
Teacher respects personal writing of student.
Teacher skims, reading what student wants to share.
Grammar & spelling aren't graded or marked.
Only one draft is written.
Teacher shares by writing too.

Variations
Students write for 5 minutes at beginning of class or 20 minutes at home.
Teacher gives topics or leaves topics open.

Figure 8–1.   Journals

What to Write On

The word *journal* connotes writing for the self. Some students keep a *diary* to record such momentous events as running into heartthrob Harry/Harrietta at the local videotape rental store. A journal differs from a diary in its emphasis on ideas, such as a newsperson's journal of important ideas that one day might go into a feature article. Another common term for a student journal is *learning log* or *log,* as in a ship's record of important events: "Wind from the N.E. 10 knots. Russian freighter to starboard. Three flying fish on deck. Small hole in the mainsail, repaired."

Note the differences in purpose. The diary is about "who I am." The journalist's journal records "what I think and what I see." And the ship's log notes conditions of the sea and the ship—the topic or subject matter of the log. People record such things because of a need to write (and, once the need creates a routinized discipline, because of a sense of guilt).

A student journal in a class, however, requires a different motivation:

To understand how I learn

To realize why I didn't understand yesterday

To celebrate finally understanding (and remembering) a particular concept

To share my excitement at finding this subject interesting

You guide students to these realizations by your suggestions of writing topics.

What do students write on? Topics can vary from the completely open to the structured and focused. Open topics generally guide students to write about the class and its topic, and about what the student is learning or, perhaps, having trouble learning. Structured topics guide students to particular questions relevant to a lesson plan. Either method will work in all content areas.

Open Topics.   A writing-to-learn journal focuses students on the course content. The team teachers referred to in the beginning of this chapter used the following simple guidelines for the daily entries: We will expect you to record your understanding of what is occurring in class each day. What is the purpose of the activity? What is adding to your understanding? What issues remain unresolved? At least once a month, you should include at least one description of an application in your daily life of what has been learned in class.

The students write their entries about the class, about how and what they learned, about confusions and successes. Ask students to tell you what you did that helped them learn most and where they felt confused. As your students share their thoughts with you, you will better sense how you achieve your successes (in terms of successful learning or of attitude change toward your subject) and where you need to alter your approach.

Structured Topics.   Teachers can provide a different topic daily to precede or follow up a class discussion. Some of these topics are reflective: How comfortable did you feel about our science experiment today? What do you see as the main idea in yesterday's lesson? Other topics are more specific: What were the effects of the bombing of Pearl Harbor on American society? What would American politics be like today if John F. Kennedy had not been assassinated?

Teachers can direct reflective writing toward the reading in the class—the textbook, a novel, or a primary source in history. Students *do not* write an outline or summary about the chapter being studied; instead, they reflect on what they found important, what they found difficult, what they would like to know more about. As such, writing becomes a direct tool for the reflective reader.

Students can also write about the class itself—an experiment in science, a class discussion, or a test. In the vocabulary chapters we noted the difference between recognition and production. Journal writing can help you with difficult vocabulary that you want your students to produce. In Chapter 6, for example, we used the short piece entitled "The Mission" as a way of getting students to think about the human costs of the Great Depression. In a journal, we might expect to see references to vocabulary taught and, in general, to the discussion in class.

In or Out of Class

Teachers successfully use journal writing in class and out. Students can write in class every day for five or ten minutes or out of class for longer time periods.

In-class journal writing has several strong advantages. First, of course, the students will write because you offer them time to do so. They cannot forget to write or find some other excuse. Second, the shared activity builds up the classroom unity and sense of trust, both of which are valuable for classroom discussion. Third, the activity gathers students' attention from their recent encounters at the lockers and refocuses it on your topic. For this reason, journal writing seems particularly effective at the beginning of each class period.

Fourth, as you will notice immediately, when you ask students to write on the topic of the day (whether you use journals or not), class discussion will be livelier and involve more students. Why? If you ask students to write for three minutes on what they see as the generalities between several animal species, categories of French words, short stories, historical events, or programming languages, each student will probably come up with one idea. The one idea might not be *the* best generalization but might be insightful and valid. If you simply ask the class for generalizations, one or two students offer their first thoughts and the others think, "Oh, Sam and Sue know the answers; my idea was probably wrong," and sit silently. But with their thoughts before them looking like real ideas because they are on paper, students are less reticent to offer their ideas.

A final advantage of in-class writing is that it allows you to write along with the students, showing them that the activity is important and giving you a way of modeling for them your own reflective thinking. Share with them occasionally what you have written—your hopes for the lesson, your fears that something was not clear yesterday, your enthusiasm for a particular idea.

Many teachers prefer students to write in their journals outside of class. Usually, students write a set number of entries per week—twenty minutes five times a week, one paragraph per day, or a half hour every three days. The advantage of out-of-class writing is that students have the chance to reflect for more than three or five minutes. The longer time allows students to become more involved with reflective writing, and their thoughts "flow" more fruitfully at the end of twenty minutes than at the beginning.

Another advantage of out-of-class writing, in some teachers' opinion, is that it does not use up the regular class time. Nonetheless, journals must in some way be dealt with during class time. Students who write outside of class need reinforcement to know that the journal is important and not just busywork. Sharing your own journal writing helps, as does offering some class time for sharing of ideas from the journals.

Another possibility is to assign students a "journal partner." Give partners time in class to share reading of their journal as an additional way to give feedback to students.

When and How Long to Use Journals

Teachers often advise limiting journals to several months out of the school year. As with any good strategy, journal writing can become old and less effective.

One way to organize journals is to use them with your first period class from October to November, with your second period class from January to February, and with your troublesome fourth period class from March to April. If you have one prep for three classes, you have feedback from students throughout the year, and you can vary how you handle the journals, trying open topics out of class for one group, in-class writing on specified topics for another. Then you can see which is more valuable for you and your students.

After They Write, What Do You Do with It?

Student journals differ vastly from traditional school writing, with different ground rules. Students write for themselves, with only the teacher or journal partner serving as the audience. It is important that the reader values the process of thinking that the student undergoes. It is a place to respect the student's ideas, to say "Thanks for sharing." It is private writing in the sense that a teacher does not read passages to the class unless permission has been granted by the writer.

Reading journal entries gives you a different experience and re-sponsibility than when you lug home a stack of 150 tenth-grade essays on mitosis. Reading student journals increases your interest in students and respect for their knowledge — and that has to result in better teaching. One caution: Teachers often find students' journals so interesting that they spend much more time reading the first set or two of journals than they expect.

Read each journal every two weeks or so; longer than two weeks will be overwhelming. Take home a percentage of journals every week or twice a week and spread out your reading.

After reading a number of stacks of journals, you will learn to vary your reading rate, skimming and scanning parts, slowing down and reread-ing others (see Chapter 10 on reading flexibility). Journal reading goes more quickly than reading essays where you have to assign a grade and make written statements of worth. Journals can be read rapidly because you are looking for the gist, for information that students are learning, for problems that students are having that you can help with, for feedback about your own teaching, and for pats on the back about your own successes.

Journal writing is first-draft writing; this is not the place to pour red ink over spelling errors and grammar problems. The primary purpose is for the student to reflect about the content of the class, and any outpouring of red ink stops this reflection immediately. Teacher evaluation must be tailored to teacher purpose, which means that journal writing is the least marked up of all writing, usually with a few simple comments, such as "I'm glad you enjoyed yesterday's class" or "Thanks for helping me understand why I didn't cover that topic as well as I wanted." Students must feel comfortable with the journal as a place where they are encouraged to think.

One mathematics teacher who uses journals asks her students if they want comments on spelling. Her rationale is, "Why should I let them write 'alot' for a whole year if telling them once might help them learn the spelling?" The logic sounds reasonable, but you must keep in mind whether you want students to learn your subject or the correct spelling of "a lot."

Most students will demand some sort of mark or grade for the effort they put into journals. The quantity-versus-quality issue is a real concern for teachers. Does a teacher set a page limit to encourage quantity, thereby punishing concise writers or causing them to fill up the page with vapidities? Does a teacher require some writing in each entry? And how does a teacher evaluate quality? Teachers debate these issues, and will continue to do so, but some solutions seem more acceptable to teachers than others. Teachers generally check off the entries with a mark of some kind, to reinforce to students that it is a requirement. Unlike a polished piece of writing, such as a report or theme, journal writing generally does not receive a letter grade.

Some teachers give the journal a certain percentage of the final grade, from 15 to 30 percent. Students receive the full credit at the beginning of the journal-keeping session but lose points for not keeping up. This grading system can help the weaker students in a class. Some teachers solve the problem of quality by assigning a weekly grade, such as:

A plus for work going beyond the guidelines

A check for work fulfilling the guidelines

A minus for work less than adequate

Each plus raises and each minus lowers the course grade by a small percentage.

You should view the short comments that you write on journals as one way of dealing with the quality issue. A "good idea" or "I'm glad you let me know about that problem" in the appropriate place can do far more to reinforce the learning you hope for in a journal than any system of checks and pluses. And, the better the comments, the more likely the students will respond with quality entries of their own.

OTHER TYPES OF REFLECTIVE WRITING

Although we have used the word *journal* throughout this discussion, we hope that you see journal writing as a *category* of nonthreatening writing— pointed toward students' learning processes rather than products. You should view such writing as a tool for generating student awareness about learning and for generating ideas—a type of writing that you do not have to read in the same kind of detail as an essay or theme. You can use this category of writing at any time. Stop during any lesson and ask the students to write for a few minutes on the idea at hand. This two or three minutes of writing generates so many ideas in a classroom that it increases participation in classroom discussion, both in quantity and quality of ideas.

Teachers who use writing-to-learn for reflection have many variations. You may enjoy reading a book in the reference list (Gere, 1985) written by teachers, in grades 7 to 12, of German, science, mathematics, English, history, art, and other subjects. In fifteen essays, these teachers describe their use of various writing-to-learn techniques. Among these techniques are anonymous notes in which a student admits what she or he didn't understand or wants to know about the lesson or the reading. The teacher reads these notes to the class in order to clarify problems in a nonthreatening way. Ask students to write you notes telling you what they think they have been studying, the main ideas, and the difficulties. "It's a wonderful way of putting you in touch with the students," one teacher reports. "You find out whether students are not paying attention because they are lost, because they don't understand, or because they are bored." The technique works especially well for the shy students who never ask the questions they may desperately want answers to.

CLOSING STATEMENT

This chapter describes a few writing-to-learn ideas that teachers find valuable. These ideas fall under a category involving reflective writing, such as journal writing, in which students write about current issues you are studying.

Journals and other reflective writing, such as anonymous notes, give you information about your students' learning and your own teaching to use in informal evaluation of your classroom. In Chapter 11, we further discuss the uses of evaluation.

Another category of writing is more public: writing that requires an audience and purpose, writing that requires help with the process of writing, writing that requires close reading and evaluation from you. We discuss ways to use this second type of writing as writing-to-learn in the next chapter.

REFERENCES

GERE, ANN RUGGLES (ED.). *Roots in the Sawdust: Writing to Learn Across the Disciplines.* Urbana, IL: National Council of Teachers of English, 1985.

MARIK, RAY. "Teaching Special Education History Using Writing-to-Learn Strategies." In Anne Ruggles Gere (Ed.), *Roots in the Sawdust: Writing to Learn Across the Disciplines.* Urbana, IL: National Council of Teachers of English, 1985.

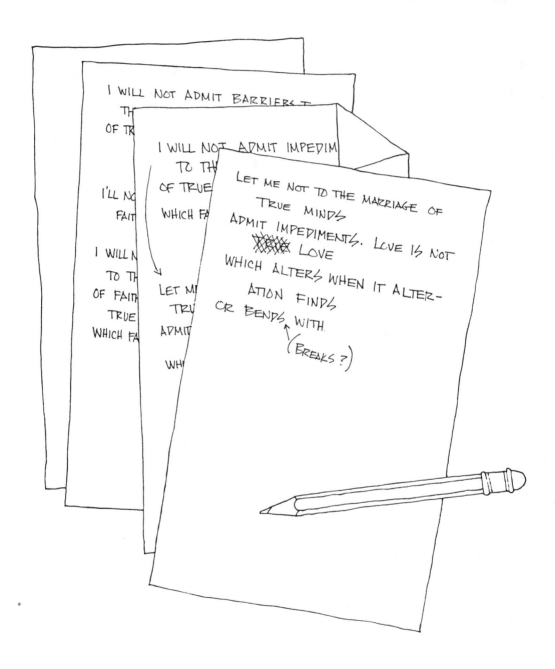

9

WRITING TO LEARN: VARIATIONS ON A THEME

Journals and other forums for reflective writing allow students to explore ideas in relative privacy, but students also need to display their knowledge in public. Content area teachers value the experience students have in writing a research paper on whales, an analysis on Huckleberry Finn, a description of a scientific process, or a review of an artwork.

In this chapter, we argue that, as with reading assignments, writing assignments need to be purposeful. Second, when your goal is public writing, students need a real or implied audience. Increasingly, teachers have realized that because much school writing is a form of communication it needs an audience: teachers, parents, other students, or a fictitious audience (Huck Finn himself). Providing an audience helps make the writing purposeful.

And third, content area teachers need an awareness of the writing process. Simply put, realization that writing is a process means that teachers and students concentrate more on the process rather than the final paper. One implication is that a real audience can help most effectively *during* writing, rather than at the end when the paper is finished and ready for grading. In order to refocus on the process rather than the product, teachers are incorporating writing groups or peer evaluation, teaching their students about prewriting and revising techniques that can help a writer along, and creating a classroom environment conducive to taking risks, being wrong, and learning.

When using peer writing groups to help the writer before the final draft, you, the teacher, benefit in that the product you ultimately see is better. However, the goal is not only a better writing product—because writing is a complicated procedure, writers learn and reflect during this process. The payoff is that the student remains engaged in your content area while working with a topic during writing.

First we will consider what a typical theme, also known as "the five-paragraph essay," lacks as a vehicle for writing-to-learn.

DEFICIENCIES OF THE FIVE-PARAGRAPH ESSAY

Traditionally the five-paragraph essay has been the format for formal or public writing in schools. Let's consider a typical essay topic and what it achieves:

> *Topic: Write About the Causes of the Civil War*
>
> Paragraph 1. State topic sentence and introduce essay.
>
> Paragraph 2. Deal with one idea relating to topic sentence.
>
> Paragraph 3. Deal with a second idea relating to topic sentence.
>
> Paragraph 4. Deal with a third idea relating to topic sentence.
>
> Paragraph 5. Restate topic sentence and three ideas.

The five-paragraph essay allows for three ideas and a few details about each. The fifth paragraph simply repeats the rest, without adding to the writer's or reader's knowledge in any way. Many students develop a formula for this type of writing and substitute it for thinking.

Notice too that the essay topic has no audience or purpose, other than "writing for the teacher for a grade." Because themes are often boring and ill-written, teachers who assign them usually do not enjoy reading them. Frequently teachers base evaluation of themes on spelling and mechanical errors which, presumably, had little role in the causes of the Civil War.

Providing an audience and purpose challenges a writer and makes the writing easier to do. Outside of school, all writing is addressed to someone for some reason—advertisements, notices of land use action, editorials, letters, resumés, novels, cookbooks, and the like. School writing can also have implied audiences and purposes, for example: You are a French traveler to America during the years before the Civil War. You have visited only Boston and are heavily influenced by the abolitionists. Write a letter to an old school friend at home about your interpretation of the causes of this upcoming war. (You don't have to write in French.)

The advantage of such a writing topic is that the subject, causes of the Civil War, is so complex that labeling a list of three causes as *The* causes trivializes our understanding of this event. In addition, opinions differ about these causes. By creating a writing topic such as the above, you design a situation in which you can learn more about a student's understanding of the event than whether he or she memorized a list in the textbook. You have given students an interesting problem to solve, and they'll have more fun writing.

AUDIENCE—WHAT IS IT?

We now need to return to the term used above—*audience*. If you listed what the word meant to you, in the context of writing, you'd probably discover that it has several meanings, as in Figure 9–1.

Each writing has a different audience. A diary is for one's self, a letter to Aunt Susan is for Aunt Susan, and a proposal to the SuperTech Company is for the powers-that-be within the company. You may write for

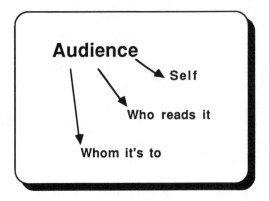

Figure 9-1. Audience in Writing

a specific audience but allow others to read it. If you work for the company that sends the proposal to SuperTech, several people will read the proposal before it leaves the office. When you write a paper, resumé, or article, you probably ask others to read it before you part with it. We might call this second group of readers *editors*—an important audience who can help us understand when we communicate poorly.

Audiences can be real or implied. A *real audience* is the person the piece is written for, such as you rereading your diary, Aunt Susan reading your letter, and someone in personnel reading your resumé. *Implied audiences* are readers who are addressed in the writing but who cannot read it because they don't exist (as with the French school friend in the Civil War example above) or because they cannot give a personal response (as in a letter to the editor).

In school writing, the teacher is usually an audience, even if the specified audience is someone else (the French friend in the Civil War example above). It used to be that students wrote primarily for teachers, on topics that the teachers already knew more about than they did (Applebee, 1981; Britton, Burgess, Martin, McLeod, and Rosen, 1975). Unsurprisingly, telling someone something they already know often results in boredom for the student/writer and the teacher/reader.

Increasingly, teachers have begun easing themselves out of the awkward position as the sole audience for school writing. They use journals and other forms of reflective writing to involve students as audiences of their own writing. They organize writing groups in their classes so that other students become the audience as well, sharing and responding to the writing as readers and editors. And they prescribe an audience (implied or real) and purpose in formal student writing.

Situational Sequencing

Situational sequencing faces the problem of purpose and audience head on and solves it by providing a series of writing topics on, essentially, the same theme. These topics work best when a sense of play is involved, as Schuster (1987) suggests. Students circle around the same topic from different points of view, usually writing to an implied audience.

For example, here is a slightly abbreviated sequence from Schuster (1987), relevant to a social studies class. Notice that it begins with a situation or scenario. Then a series (or sequence) of numbered writing topics follow. Each writing topic would be given individually, separated by a few days or a week.

You are walking through the aisles of your local grocery store, looking for tuna, soup, and brussels sprouts. As you turn the corner of aisle 3, you see an old woman ahead of you. Her clothes are ragged, her hair unkempt, her face gaunt. She is what you would call a "street person" or a "bag lady," poor and homeless. You observe her taking a can of green beans and sticking it inside her torn coat.

1. What do you do? Consider the various possibilities available to you, and then describe which one you would follow.

2. You are the store manager. Sitting in your office is an old woman who has been accused of shoplifting by a student who has given eyewitness testimony. You have had a lot of shoplifting in your store and you want it to end. But you are also aware that the old woman might be starving. Before you call the police, you decide to talk to this woman. Create the conversation that would occur between you (the manager) and the old woman.

3. It is a week later. You (the student) have been thinking about the incident quite a bit and have decided to write a letter to the editor about the situation. You can take any point of view that seems appropriate. Write that letter.

4. The subject of "hunger in America" interests you enough that you decide to do some research. You consult the *Reader's Guide* to locate some recent articles on this subject. On notecards, hand in three citations of articles you think would be interesting. Include all the necessary information so you can look up the articles later in the week.

Notice that these four writing topics are ordered from what the student already knows best ("What do you do?") to more distant sources of knowledge (the *Reader's Guide*). Notice too that the first topic is reflective, written for the student, as in a journal writing. The second allows for a fictional audience in the creative dialog that reflects understanding of human interactions and values. The third has an implied audience, a letter to the editor of a newspaper, thereby giving students a model of the style of writing usually done for such letters. The fourth has no audience and involves no writing, per se, but it sends the students to do preliminary research which may result in further thinking and writing about the topic.

Each of the four topics in this example is related to a central theme — in this case, hunger in the United States — and each allows the student to re-see the complex issues. Generally, situational sequences are short and quickly written. You can use five to seven writing topics during a unit lasting several weeks. Students do not have time to polish and rewrite each piece. Yet, they are "revising" in the sense that "revision" means "to re-see." Each part of the sequence shows growth in the student's thinking. Therefore, your grades are based not on polished papers and grammatical perfection but on students' ideas.

Point of view is the key to situational sequencing. Students deepen their understanding by grappling with the connections and opposites that your sequences place in front of them. Situational sequencing, like journal writing, is another technique developed for learning-to-write classes. It lends itself well to *any* course in which thinking is the goal.

Thus, our previous Civil War example about the French traveler to America before the Civil War can be one of a series in the sequence, perhaps the first, and the series can continue depending on your goals in the course, tying in the student's own experience and feelings with the historical event and leading to research and more reading.

You will probably have realized that situational sequencing topics lend themselves well to journal writing. They are also helpful when your goal is building toward production of vocabulary, deepening students' understanding of the technical language in your field, as discussed in Chapters 4 and 5. The sense of play in the topics keeps students interested in writing and you interested in reading.

Real Audiences (Besides You)

Researchers in San Diego (Cohen and Riel, 1986; Riel, 1986) studied the effect of real audiences — students from other cities or countries — on students' writing. On a computer network, students wrote to each other from California, Israel, Alaska, Japan, and other distant locations. Seventh graders in Jerusalem wrote better for their California peers than for their teachers, Riel and Cohen (1986) found, suggesting that a real audience helps the quality of students' writing. But real audiences help with writing-to-learn as well. Students learn about culture (Riel, 1986), as when Japanese and Californian students discovered to their surprise that each had a Disneyland. They trade facts about science, as when students shared and traded observations about Halley's Comet or water conservation.

Part of the value of a real audience is that students share facts in a purposeful and meaningful way, encountering new ways of thinking from the audience. Another part is that explaining something clearly in writing helps us understand better, or helps us understand what we don't understand. As teachers, we know that the best way to learn something is to teach it. Students with real audiences are put in a similar position.

You don't need a classroom full of computers and modems to allow writing to real audiences; real audiences already sit in your class. Form the students into groups, calling them "writing groups," "peer evaluation groups," or whatever you wish. These groups, consisting of three or four students, should meet regularly to share ideas about and drafts of their writing, and as such they become a support group. Three members might be optimal for short typical class period slots of time, but absenteeism might make the groups too small. A group of five is too large because it risks letting the quiet students become overlooked.

Students in a writing group help each other clarify their ideas, and the small-group activity encourages good work from each individual. Writing groups are valuable because writing is hard work. Writing for a public audience still involves basic writing competencies and organization of ideas in a readable manner. A student writing group shares writing in draft form, rather than finished essays. As such, the writers receive help and encour-

agement during the writing stage, when it is more useful, rather than after the writing is over and the grade given.

Teachers report successes with writing groups in classes from seventh to twelfth grades, in all varieties of schools. But success with writing groups does not happen instantly. First, teachers need to build a community spirit in the classroom—a spirit of mutual respect. Ground rules and teacher observation are needed to protect students from attack. Each writer needs to be told where and how he or she did well. The group has to become independent, but it also needs to be well managed, with equal time for each participant (a watch can help so that one student does not get all the time). Also, if a student has not prepared work, that student should not be allowed in the group that day; each individual has the dual responsibility as a writer and as a responder.

Here is an example of a procedure for writing groups. Variations have been used in many classrooms. The groups are formed and remain together for the year, if possible.

1. At the beginning of each session, the students divide the time by the number of participants and make sure that all students have an equal amount of time for their selection.

2. The writer reads the selection aloud, without comment, while the others listen.

3. After the writer stops, the listeners make a few notes on their overall impression.

4. The writer rereads the selection while the others take notes about specifics they might want to comment on, both positive and negative.

5. Going around the group, each listener in turn shares comments on the selection. The writer listens but does not make excuses.

This highly structured procedure works much better than telling students simply to "talk about your writing." The structure helps students know what to do and keeps them on task. Each has a role to play as reader and listener, including reading, listening, note taking, and offering comments. It protects them from worrying about being unduly attacked. Because they read their writing aloud, rather than share written drafts, their listeners cannot be distracted from the content by spelling errors. The groups need to be regularly scheduled, because at first students will have little to say about the writing. Their confidence as listeners and as responders needs to be built up over time by experience. The writer (reader) particularly needs to refrain from excuses (Elbow, 1973); later drafts are a better, more efficient way for the writer to incorporate responses.

Is it fair to have students share their writing? Some of us see writing as a solitary activity, hard work to be rewarded or punished with a grade and a smattering of red ink. But is that the best way to learn? Much of published, business, and technical writing is collaborative, in a sense. Writers brainstorm together, write and revise together, or at least have others read their drafts. It is unusual for an article or book to be published without changes made by editors. A writing group acts like an editorial group but, more importantly in the content area, it shares ideas.

Having a real audience benefits you, the teacher, in that the papers you ultimately do read are of better quality, making your job more enjoyable. But more than the quality of writing, students share ideas. One study (Gere and Abbott, 1985) taped students' writing groups at varying secondary grade levels over a period of time to see what students talked about. The study found that students remained on-task in writing groups and that the majority of students' comments were on the content of the writing. Therefore, although writing groups originated to help students "write," they become important discussion tools in content area classes. In discussing their writing, students share ideas about your content area.

THE WRITING PROCESSES

What does a content area teacher need to know about the writing process? Good writing seldom occurs without prethought and reworking. For example, Hemingway rewrote the last line of A *Farewell to Arms* thirty-nine times, and scientists often rewrite articles and grant proposals to respond to requirements of their audiences. Unfortunately, however, we usually make students write under the gun in school writing. Observational studies of ninth and eleventh grade classes found that the time between the giving of an assignment and when students begin to write is three minutes (Applebee, 1981, p. 96). Incorporating planning for the writing process in your classroom can improve the quality of the work and keep students thinking about your topic longer than the typical three minutes of "prewriting" time.

It has become customary to think of the writing process as having three parts—prewriting, planning, and revision. The three parts are logical when we think of prewriting as the time between an assignment (or idea for writing) and the writing and of rewriting as the time after the writing is finished. In practice, however, thinking about writing in terms of a stage of three parts can lead us into trouble. Writing processes—or techniques for writing—will not fit into neat little boxes for two reasons. First, no two people seem to use the same "process" (Betza, 1987), and second, anything a writer can do in one of the three prewriting, writing, and revising boxes can also be done in the other two boxes.

The writing styles of people are vastly different. Some people appear to spend much of their time in one of the three stages. Students traditionally ignore the prewriting and revising stage (and no wonder, if they are allowed only three minutes to prewrite). Some professionals are said to spend 90 percent of their writing time in planning or prewriting. A writing teacher who reviewed this manuscript commented, "I'm no pro, but at least 75 percent of my total time is spent [in planning]. My teachers always thought I was daydreaming!"

Others revise extensively. But when we try to associate specific techniques with a stage or box, we cannot make it work. A good example comes from research on writing. One well-known teacher of writing and professional writer, Donald Murray, has written at length about the extensive role that *revision* plays in his composing process. A researcher (Berkenkotter, 1983) observed Murray's composing process for several months. When she began to categorize specific techniques, she found that many were categorized as both planning and revising. She recategorized all of the activities as *planning*, redefining the composing process of this writer as primarily extensive planning with little revision. So much for the value of labels.

It would be nice if we could find a writing process that produces good writing, but unfortunately such different processes produce both good and bad writing that it is difficult to tell students how to write. As soon as we force students to write one draft, we limit those who need to revise. As soon as we require students to follow a particular sort of prewriting technique, such as listening or outlining, we intrude on the methods that other students like to use.

Outlining is a good example. One researcher (Emig, 1971), who wrote to famous people to find out how many use outlines before writing fiction and nonfiction, found that only about 10 percent used this technique. Yet at the time of her research teachers routinely forced 100 percent of their students to create formal outlines before writing. (Some still do.) Although a few students like formal outlining as a prewriting technique and thankfully remember the teacher who taught them, most do not.

Our second argument is that the three boxes, or categories, have little meaning in terms of writing strategies, such as outlining, reading, thinking, or discussing. For example, the techniques in the following list are generally pegged as "prewriting." Many of these methods are typically taught only as prewriting techniques, as with outlining and brainstorming.

Some Techniques Often Pegged as "Prewriting"

brainstorming	questioning	reading
listing	researching	clustering
note taking	interviewing	mapping
outlining	thinking	role playing
discussing	dialoging	imagining
drawing		

In reality, we sometimes get stuck after writing and need to begin again. "Your resumé doesn't do you justice," a friend tells you after reading the new resumé you just paid to have copied professionally. "Let's brainstorm about other things you've done. Remember the rules—no right and wrong answers yet."

When we pointed out what we might call the Composing Process Box Fallacy to a group of teachers, many of them, thinking about their own writing, realized that they use outlining *after* writing. When a paper for a college class, for example, doesn't seem right, some people create an outline from their paper to see where their organization went wrong. Thus, when we teach one or two techniques as "prewriting," we limit students from the vast repertoire of techniques.

You will notice from the previous listing of the so-called prewriting techniques that they are also among those we discuss in other chapters as reading techniques—also not limited to pre-, during, or postreading. In this book we emphasize a three-part lesson plan involving prereading, during reading, and postreading (in particular, see Chapter 12). We argue that most good reading techniques can be used at any stage. Good questions are helpful before, during, and after reading, as are discussion, prediction, skimming, writing, and so on. We propose a similar analogy with the writing process, typically viewed as before, during, and after writing, or prewriting, writing, and revising. Too often we associate brainstorming with a stage (i.e., planning before we write). Students need to know that brainstorming and many other techniques can also help them during and after writing. That is why we call it the "writing process<u>es</u>."

Techniques Content Area Teachers Find Beneficial

As we suggested in Chapter 8, a book you might enjoy reading is *Roots in the Sawdust* (Gere, 1985), a collection of essays written by secondary teachers using writing-to-learn techniques in all content areas. You will notice that many strategies work equally well in different areas. Although there are many techniques useful in writing-to-learn, we will briefly discuss four that content area teachers seem to find most beneficial. These four— brainstorming, listing, clustering, and mapping—work well when combined in a class period or over several days.

Brainstorming and listing help students come up with ideas about what they know (about South America, about the circulatory system, about surrealism, etc.) before beginning a unit on these ideas. Clustering and mapping help organize the ideas, so that students structure the details into concepts. When manipulating ideas to find relationships, students understand and remember concepts better. In Chapter 5, for example, we propose a word sort as a postreading vocabulary exercise when the goal is seeing relationships among major concepts. Sorting, clustering, and manipulating activities are just as helpful for writing, helping writers find and re-see ideas.

Lists and clustering can grow out of journals for essay writing, not vice versa. Teachers use many strategies together, from lists to extended writing, and not necessarily in that order. For example, the whole class might brainstorm ideas about a topic, then select ideas from it relevant to a single focus.

We recommend that you introduce these techniques as whole-class activities, but after your writing groups seem to be independent, use the small groups as places to try out the techniques on a continual basis. When brainstorming in a whole class, everyone benefits from seeing the many ideas that emerge. But in a small group, everyone has more opportunity to offer ideas himself or herself, and the chances for involvement are greater. On days when students have drafts to share, use the procedures we outlined earlier for writing groups, but on days when students are beginning to choose topics, to think about issues, or to solve problems, have the groups try out some of these techniques.

CLOSING STATEMENT

Your role is not to teach writing any more than it is to teach reading. Just as we will urge you in Chapter 10 to consider what reading study strategies you might find helpful to share with your students, we suggest that you select helpful strategies with the writing process that you can use in class. Knowing how to use "the writing process" is as helpful as knowing how to use "the reading process."

Just as you cannot spend all of your time teaching reading or study strategies (or you will never get to mathematics or physics or social studies), you cannot spend all of your time teaching writing techniques. Our advice is to select a few methods and offer them to students. Avoid a scattershot approach. Students will have to make decisions themselves whether to use a given technique or not, as appropriate for the particular writing they need to do.

We see writing as a powerful tool for learning, for thinking, and for reflection in the classroom. It is a tool for inquiry of a writer's own knowledge. (See Chapter 10 for a different use of writing, as a study strategy.) During drafting and discussing in writing groups, you have a tool for informal evaluation, as we will talk about more in Chapter 11. Patience helps with writing-to-learn; results don't come instantly, but their form is refreshingly different from a stack of five-paragraph essays.

REFERENCES

APPLEBEE, ARTHUR N. *Writing in the Secondary School: English and the Content Areas.* Urbana, IL: National Council of Teachers of English, 1981.

BERKENKOTTER, CAROL. "Decisions and Revisions: The Planning Strategies of a Publishing Writing," *College Composition and Communication, 34,* 1983, 156–167.

BETZA, RUTH E. "Rhetorical Awareness in Word Level Revision of College Writers." Unpublished dissertation, Seattle, WA: University of Washington, 1987.

BRITTON, JAMES; BURGESS, TONY; MARTIN, NANCY; MCLEOD, ALEX; AND ROSEN, HAROLD. *The Development of Writing Abilities (11–18).* Houndsmills, UK: Macmillan Education, 1975.

COHEN, MOSHE, AND RIEL, MARGARET. *Computer Networks: Creating Real Audiences for Students' Writing.* Report 15. La Jolla, CA: Center for Human Information Processing, University of California, San Diego, 1986.

ELBOW, PETER. *Writing Without Teachers.* London: Oxford University Press, 1973.

EMIG, JANET. *The Composing Processes of Twelfth Graders.* Urbana, IL: National Council of Teachers of English, 1971.

GERE, ANNE RUGGLES (ED.). *Roots in the Sawdust: Writing to Learn Across the Disciplines.* Urbana, IL: National Council of Teachers of English, 1985.

GERE, ANNE RUGGLES, AND ABBOTT, ROBERT D. "Thinking About Writing: The Language of Writing Groups," *Research in the Teaching of English, 19,* 1985, 362–385.

RIEL, MARGARET. *The Educational Potential of Computer Networking.* Report 16. La Jolla, CA: Center for Human Information Processing, University of California, San Diego, 1986.

SCHUSTER, CHARLES I. "The Power of Play," *The Clearing House, 60,* 1987, 296–299.

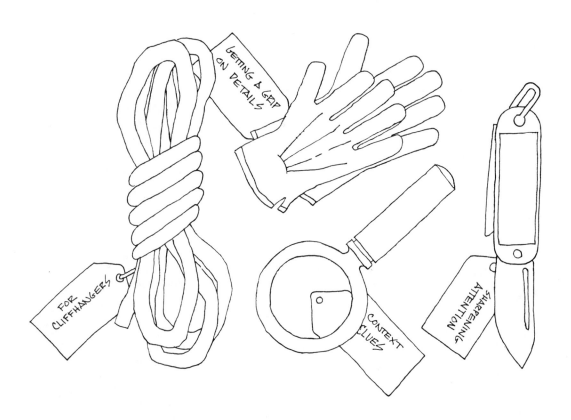

10
STUDY SKILLS

In the transition periods of schooling, from elementary to middle or junior high and from junior high to high school, students and their teachers worry about whether the students have the skills necessary to survive in the new and, presumably, more academically demanding environment. It is in these transition periods that study skills are typically taught.

The instruction is given and students get whatever there is to get and move on, succeeding to one degree or another in the new environment. But study skills are more than devices to get through transitions. They are necessary at virtually all levels of schooling, and although they do not need to be a large part of the curriculum they do need to be taught, used, and reviewed within the various content areas at all levels.

Study skills give students a degree of independence and enable them to get more out of reading. Teaching study skills is not your main thrust, but if you select a few strategies relevant to your content area and spend a few class periods teaching them, you and your students will profit from the time spent.

COMMONALITIES OF FORMALIZED
STUDY SKILLS SYSTEMS

There are many study skills and we do not intend to provide a cookbook of all of them. Before we present a few formalized systems, we want to point out that most formalized study systems involve five elements:

1. Purpose

2. Preview

3. Read

4. Review with book

5. Review without book

We have already discussed at length purpose setting and techniques for prereading, reading, and postreading instruction.

Purpose

We have argued repeatedly that purpose for reading is the teacher's responsibility, and that the student should be aware of the teacher's purpose. In the context of study skills, the purpose should additionally involve students' awareness of the type of testing expected from the reading. That is, will the test be essay, true/false, multiple choice, or short answer? Each type of test requires a different type of studying, depending on the emphasis on literal or factual recall or inferential and higher-than-inferential thinking.

Preview

Preview means that a student does something with the text before reading it, and this something can take as little as a few minutes. Skimming and scanning for headings and sampling bits of text are excellent methods of previewing, both of which we discuss later in this chapter. In Chapter 2, we suggested that if you give the class sixty seconds to skim a new chapter, they will be able to tell you a great deal of the gist of the chapter. That is the reason for previewing—to gain an idea of the gist or direction of a passage or chapter.

Another excellent preview technique is prediction, as we discussed in Chapters 6 and 7. With prediction, students read the title or some of the headings and ask themselves where they think the chapter will go. Such an activity increases the students' involvement with the text.

In other chapters of this book we suggested many classroom activities related to reading. Here, however, the goal is to encourage students to use study skills on their own, independently. We can easily allow a few class periods to illustrate prediction or skimming and scanning, but how do we know that students will adopt these methods on their own? We don't, and this is the difficulty with teaching study skills. We believe that you will be most successful in the least amount of time if you design your sessions on study skills so that students will see for themselves that they learn and retain more by skimming first than by reading once, word-for-word. Have your students read two passages of equal length, one with some sort of prereading and one without. Then give a short quiz. If students do better on the quiz after using a prereading technique, they will be more likely to adopt the method on their own.

Reading

When we go home after a hard day and pick up a mystery novel or watch a sitcom on TV, we probably don't care much if we remember the next day what we read or watched. But with studying, we care very much.

Therefore, our purpose heavily influences the way we read. Perhaps you have told students to understand the main relationships between two types of animals because they will have an essay test on it, for example. We have heard of a junior high student who read science fiction for facts, misunderstanding the purpose of science fiction.

Readers need to vary their rate of reading according to their purpose and the difficulty of reading material. If you begin to observe students reading silently in class, you might notice that some students who seem less able to retain information from text plod word-for-word through a passage with the same rate of reading, despite the purpose and difficulty of the passage. Making students aware of their own reading rate can help. They should know that "the faster, the better" is not necessarily true with study reading.

In addition to varying their rate of reading, students need to reread when necessary. Students who do not actively monitor their comprehension will continue reading even when they are no longer understanding. Retention for a test is impossible under such conditions.

Perhaps most important, students need to acquire the habit of reminding themselves of their purpose for reading.

Review with the Book

In reviewing with the book, the student goes through a similar procedure as previewing with skimming and scanning. Here, students ask themselves, "Do I understand what this boldface print refers to?" If they don't, they re-read, but if they do, they go on. Essentially, they skim to see what they recognize.

Review without the Book

The final phase is a kind of pretest for students, to assess their own ability to remember what they read and therefore their own preparation for a class discussion or a test. Many strategies are possible here. Students can recall mentally or in writing all that they remember. The simplest way is to close the book and recall as much as possible.

If your goal is to establish relationships among concepts, then the students would do well to organize what they remember in a kind of outline or map. These outlines and maps can be quite informal; the goal is for the student to recall details but to juxtapose them in sensible ways. They will retain more by restructuring knowledge.

In a sense, journal writing can be an informal way of reviewing without the text, particularly if students become used to writing about what they read. Generally they will pick a main idea that interested or confused them.

LEVELS OF STUDY READING

We reiterate that students need to become independent with study skills, and they become so more easily when they understand clearly what is expected of them. Tests composed of scattershot and unimportant literal questions will not help students study for main ideas, because if they do, they will score poorly on the tests. In order to help students study in your class, we propose three levels of study reading. *Study reading*, as used here, means reading in response to carefully thought out and explained reading assignments for any class. It is reading-to-learn, reading for which background has been given and for which purpose is understood. Here, again, purpose is paramount. Sections, chapters, and even books vary not only in content and concept density but also in their importance to the overall course of study. It is important that you explain this three-level, additive scheme to students so that they can adapt the level to their purpose for reading.

Level One

Level one represents broad background reading. This level of study reading suits such purposes as an overview to be followed by a lecture on the topic, or perhaps a review of a prerequisite course. Specifically, level one reading involves reading the preview and the review of the chapter (if available) and then reading the chapter itself at a pace that is brisk but comfortable. The goal, after all, is not mastery of the material but simply to become familiar, in a recognition sense, with the topic.

Level Two

Level two is for more specific information where the goal is not full retention of a lot of detail, complex sequence, or cause-and-effect relationships. Level two reading includes level one, since this is an additive process, but in addition, students skim using the chapter section and subsection headings and sampling a sentence or two from each paragraph. When that is done, students read the material carefully, with frequent reference to the purpose for reading. Level two reading is suitable for building and maintaining deeper background knowledge, for material that is important but not terribly detailed or concept heavy. As you will see, level two reading is a prelude to level three reading which is flat-out, hard work study reading.

Level Three

Level three is work. This is essentially level two reading, but in addition, students take two kinds of notes. The first is a general outline that students make after reading the chapter preview or review and while skimming as described above. Then, as the students carefully and thoroughly read, they flesh out this outline with explanations, responses, and (as needed) definitions in their own language. Level three reading is best used for detailed material where the purpose is understanding and retention of detail, cause-and-effect chains, sequences of events, and/or the thorough understanding of a complex argument or point of view. It is particularly useful for a chapter or section crucial for thorough understanding of succeeding chapters or sections.

A word of caution. There is a tendency for teachers to see all their reading assignments as needing this level of attention. They don't. To put it into immediate perspective, when we use this book in a secondary reading course at the University of Washington, we require level three reading of only Chapter 1 since that is, essentially, the backbone and reference point for everything else in the book as we teach it. Your instructor may disagree.

The three levels of study reading are suggested for use only in combination with carefully wrought reading assignments. Where those prior assumptions are not met, the study reading scheme laid out here is less likely to be successful.

SYSTEMATIC STUDY METHODS

Systematic study methods, of which SQ3R (Robinson, 1961) is probably the oldest and most familiar, are problematic at best. For one thing, the results of research testing the comparative worth of the various methods against one another and, in some cases, against no specific study skills instruction at all, reveal mixed to negative findings. Using SQ3R as an example, according to Johns and McNamara (1980), articles advocating its use are "based mainly on favorable opinion." For another thing, the experience of one of the authors of this book as a secondary school teacher and reading specialist suggests that when SQ3R (or any of the letter/numeral methods) is introduced, the focus tends to be more on form than function. We refer to this as the Sentence Diagramming Syndrome. Whatever benefits, if any, might be derived from sentence diagramming are lost because the focus tends to be on the neatness of the diagram, not whether the words were correctly identified by their use in the sentence. The same thing has happened with systematic study skills instruction. Knowing the steps and getting the parts down on paper has tended to receive the attention of the teacher—not whether the system has produced better learning, retention, understanding, integration, or whatever. We have a third objection: The methods are simply too inflexible. It seems obvious that not all reading assignments should be or need to be read in the same way. Purpose varies, as we have tried to show in the previous section. No such flexibility is apparent in the various systematic study skills methods.

Nonetheless, systematic study methods are important for a number of reasons: (1) they continue to get attention in professional journals; (2) they seem to be institutionalized, lack of supporting research evidence notwithstanding; and (3) they seem to have, in short, some intuitive appeal. Therefore, they deserve a closer look.

SQ3R

SQ3R (Robinson, 1961) will serve as our guide. SQ3R stands for Survey, Question, Read, Recite, and Review. These steps are explained below.

Survey. The reader previews the material by skimming (as described on page 147) in order to get an overview of the material.

Question. The reader creates questions based on the overview, questions that he or she has determined from the overview will be answerable from the reading.

Read. The reader reads for answers to the questions posed.

Recite. The reader answers, on paper or out loud, the questions posed previously.

Review.   The reader clarifies questions not answered or not answered clearly and other possible points of confusion by rereading the relevant sections.

As previously noted, such an approach is relatively inflexible. That is, it is not in any obvious way mediated by purpose. Note, however, that purpose could be made part of the survey step. If that were the case, then this (and a host of other similar systems) would share the elements described in the three-level approach described earlier. Those elements are:

1. Purpose setting

2. Preview

3. Reading related to purpose and preview

4. Some kind of check on whether purpose was served

5. A formal method of review related to purpose

For those of you who are mad for acronyms, we offer PIRACY. A clearly stated and understood purpose is prerequisite to PIRACY.

Preview.   The student skims the material (as described on page 147) with purpose clearly in mind, perhaps even written out on paper and in plain sight.

Introspection.   The student asks himself or herself, "From my own understanding of purpose, from my own preview, and from my own background, what do I already know about this topic?"

Read.   The student reads at whatever level (see pages 141–142) best serves the purpose.

Analyze.   The student asks himself or herself, "What did I add to my previous understanding of this topic?"

Contemplate.   The student asks himself or herself, "Was my purpose served?" (If not, be prepared to commit another act of PIRACY.)

Yodel.   It's good for the soul, clears the brain (and the room), and we needed it for the acronym!

Acronyms are fun to play with, but the point remains—clear purpose related to prior experience produces purposeful, successful, and engaged reading and study.

SPEED AND FLEXIBILITY OF READING

As we mentioned earlier, good readers vary their rate of reading, whether for study or leisure purposes. We will now discuss this further, first taking up speed, then flexibility.

Forty thousand words per minute — a phenomenal speed. At this rate you could read *Gone With The Wind* in twelve minutes (Witty, 1969). Is that possible? Better question, is it desirable? Not wishing to keep you in suspense, we will answer — probably not. The answer to the first question depends on what is meant by reading. The answer to the second question is largely one of personal philosophy. From our perspective, we can see little value in reading *Gone With The Wind* or, for that matter, any other work of decent fiction in twelve minutes unless you simply wanted to say that you had read it.

Still, speed of reading is an important question, particularly with nonfiction. Flexibility is also important — choosing different rates and/or styles for different purposes. Pearson and Tierney (1984) report that high school students believe that good readers read quickly without rereading, in a minimum amount of time with maximum retention. Speed and flexibility are, in contrast to many students' beliefs, the bases for study skills and that is what this section is about.

Speed

According to Witty (1969), it is not hard to find claims of rates as high or higher than the aforementioned 40,000 words per minute. At that rate, as previously noted, you could get through a large novel in twelve minutes or so. We think it's time for a little perspective here. While cheerfully admitting that eye-hand coordination is not his strong suit and, equally cheerfully conceding that practice might improve his performance, one of us found that he could not turn the pages of a book at the speed that would be required for 40,000 words per minute. No reading at all — just page turning — and he couldn't do it. So much for the high end of what is possible.

The average, reasonably fluent adult, reading material that is not terribly complex and not terribly exotic (out of the individual's range of experience), reads somewhere in the neighborhood of 250 to 400 words per minute. That is roughly one minute per page of average type size and line length such as you might find in a paperback novel. That is the very rough average. If we consider that fluent readers typically have every word on the page in clear visual acuity, it appears that around 900 wpm is the upper physiological limit of rate (McConkie and Rayner, 1975). That is, the eyes simply do not move any faster than that.

The phenomenal speeds alluded to earlier are most likely the result of text sampling—not reading in the sense of reading all the words on the page. Text sampling, which we shall refer to as either *skimming* or *scanning,* is an important skill. It is important in two ways: knowing how to do it and, perhaps most important, knowing when to do it. But before we get to that, there is another important aspect of speed—too slow.

Rate of reading at the low end of the range has received some attention in the reading research literature, both directly and indirectly. Directly, it has been shown that where speed falls below 60 or so wpm, comprehension is severely diminished or nonexistent. Keep in mind that 60 wpm is a painfully slow rate. Even beginning readers decoding somewhat laboriously are likely to surpass 60 wpm (see Witty, 1969). At that rate all the information carried by context is lost due to the limitations of short-term memory. In effect, each word is treated as a single unit, and so nothing is "chunked" into ideas or thoughts. Indirectly, the literature suggests that where rates are terribly low, attention (which you will recall from Chapter 1 is unidirectional and finite) is totally given over to decoding and there is none left for processing meaning.

Thus, rate of reading is important but rather largely misunderstood. We think Woody Allen put the speed issue in perspective when he claimed to have taken a speed reading course that allowed him to read *War and Peace* in twenty minutes. Of that great novel, he said, "It's about Russia." Good speed, low comprehension. Painfully low rates, on the other hand, destroy comprehension and are probably symptomatic of a severe inability to decode or some other problem needing the attention of a reading specialist.

Flexibility

Reading flexibility refers to altering rate or choosing a text sampling technique appropriate for the purpose for which the reading is being done. Purpose dictates approach, which again reaffirms the importance of purpose. Where purpose is not stated or is not understood, it is obvious that no informed choice of rate or text sampling technique can be made. What choices are available?

Scanning. In most cases text sampling strategies are already in place to some greater or lesser degree, and students just need to be reminded that they have these skills and then given a bit of supervised practice and instruction. For example, if you were to look up our names in a phone directory, you wouldn't just start with the A section and read until you came to Betza or Standal. Rather, you would find the B section then *Be* or the S section then *St*, and so on until you found the name. That is scanning. Scanning is, generally, the rapid search through material for the answer to a specific, literal-level question. It is a skill students use often. A more pertinent example involves the use of a book's index. Assume for a moment that you need to know for a biology class what the letters DNA stand for. You would go to the index of your text, find the page or pages where DNA is discussed, locate that page, and *scan* for the answer to that question. Reading the entire chapter would also reveal the answer, but it wouldn't be nearly as efficient and it certainly wouldn't suit the purpose.

Skimming. The other text sampling technique already mentioned is skimming. Skimming is leafing through a chapter, section, or entire text in order to get a feel for its contents. An example may serve to clarify the concept. Suppose you have just gotten a home computer. You've done a few things with it and feel pretty comfortable in using it. But you know there is more you could do. You take yourself to a good comprehensive book store in search of a book that will give you some help. To your dismay, you find a great many books on the subject. Most likely, to choose the best one for your purposes, you'll *skim* some number of likely candidates. That is, you'll sample a bit of the text throughout in order to get a general idea of the book's contents. If you are a really good *skimmer* and you have read the introduction to the text use chapter in this book (Chapter 2), you'll probably consult the table of contents, the foreword, the chapter organization, the index, and any appendixes included, as well as sampling a bit of the text throughout. That is skimming. Skimming, as stated above, is a rapid sampling of text for the purpose of getting a general idea of its contents. A school-based example from your own background might include your recollection of skimming an assigned chapter in a text in order to better budget your study time, or perhaps the panicked riffling of assigned pages you sometimes see just before a test or quiz.

Skimming and scanning are essential study skills. They are worth introducing and practicing in class using class materials.

OTHER STUDY STRATEGIES

Traditional study strategies involve outlining, underlining, and note taking. Underlining and highlighting, in particular, seem to fit solely under the reading component in our generalized scheme of study skills. We have separated them from the others because we feel they can also be useful as preview and reviewing with the book. We also realize that many students are unable to use underlining and highlighting because they do not own their textbooks and thus are not allowed to write in them.

Outlining

We have already suggested the use of outlining as part of level three study reading. The value of outlining as a study strategy is, at least at first glance, not terribly well established. Anderson and Armbruster (1984), in their extensive review of the literature on studying, reach back to 1930 and 1935 for studies supporting the value of outlining as a study strategy. They suggest that more recent research does not support the use of this technique. They note, however, that the more recent studies may have taught students only superficial outlining skills. Again, as in the discussion of systematic study skills methods, focus on form and not on function may have been the problem. Vacca and Vacca (1986) argue, "As a study technique, outlining strategies can be used to facilitate a careful analysis and synthesis of the relations in content material." It is difficult for us to imagine that outlining has a general value as a *single* study skill. And the research seems to support that point of view. However, informal outlining as part of a more complete study approach does seem to have value.

Informal outlining is not the classic Roman numeral and upper- and lower-case letter kind, but a less formal kind focusing on symbolic representation of information and information relationships. This type of outlining does have value when, as we have said, the purpose for reading demands understanding and retention of detail, cause-and-effect chains, sequence, and/or the thorough understanding of a complex argument or point of view. When that is the case, simple outlines derived from chapter headings, section headings, and key word explanations are useful. (See Chapter 2 on text use and introduction for a more complete discussion of text organization aids.)

Students should be reminded that a good outline is an abstract representation of what was read. It is not a substitute. It is more in the way of a mnemonic. If complex text could be reduced to and successfully represented by an outline, that is the way complex text would be written. That, you will note, is not the case.

Underlining

Underlining (or highlighting) is the most frequently used study aid (Anderson and Armbruster, 1984). When students own their own texts (and, sadly enough, in many cases when they don't), underlining is their first choice of study aid. Its value is varied, again, according to purpose for reading and how well that purpose is understood and varied according to who does the outlining. Anderson and Armbruster state, "the primary facilitative effect of underlining occurs when the student generates the underlining, presumably because of the amount of processing required to make the decision about what to underline" (page 666).

Referring once more to purpose and the various levels of study reading (page 141) and also to Chapter 2 on text use, it seems that when purpose dictates it and the text allows it, student underlining (or highlighting) can prove beneficial. A word of caution, however. Anyone who has purchased a used text that has been underlined by the previous owner may have noticed a few things. One, you didn't agree with what was underlined. That is, what the previous owner deemed important didn't seem all that important to you. (That might be due as much to differences in emphasis between instructors as differences in perceived importance of text underlined.) Two, the previous owner underlined everything and, therefore, the underlining had virtually no meaning. What that suggests is that in cases where your students are allowed and encouraged to underline their texts, a little monitoring is in order. It is a simple matter to glance at a text to see if the underlining is sensible. It if is not, show the student what you would have underlined. It will be a big help.

Note Taking

Use of note taking in practice varies considerably for content area. For example, Applebee's (1981) study on secondary schools found that in social science classes observed, students were taking notes 39 percent of the time that the researchers observed the classrooms, in comparison with less than 6 percent of the time for foreign language classes.

Note taking can have the same pitfalls as underlining. Students need guidance in selecting main ideas, based on the purpose. As with underlining, you can help by spending a few sessions throughout the year monitoring and giving suggestions on note taking. You can take notes on a

mini-lecture you will give, hand them out to students, and explain why you noted what you did. In a subsequent exercise, students can take notes during one of your mini-lectures and then compare their notes in a small group and discuss their selections of important ideas and details.

CLOSING STATEMENT

A rich and varied research history exists on study skill methods. As a general rule, use of study skills shows great gains but *not* after a long time. That is, if students are not continually using them, the gains go away.

The methods suffer from a pervasive problem—as did, for example, the sentence diagram that you may remember from your own schooling. At some point the teacher forgot that you were using sentence diagrams for language learning and began grading on the diagram itself. The same danger exists with study skills. We can too easily end up grading the quality of an outline or for a rigid following of a formalized study skills system. The goal is to study, not to check for all five components. These methods are worth telling students about, but if you become more interested in whether the student has done the three Rs in SQ3R, the system is not individual enough. A formalized system is not necessary for all reading, and a formalized study skills method can be inflexible. Students need such systems particularly when they find material difficult.

The best available evidence about successful studying suggests that it involves an interplay among four variables: knowledge of the task, the kind of material being studied, the student's relevant background knowledge, and the strategies used by the student to learn the material (Anderson and Armbruster, 1984).

We have given those four variables slightly different names and discussed them a bit more broadly in this chapter and throughout the book. For instance, "knowledge of the task" is essentially what we have referred to as *purpose setting*. Anderson and Armbruster discuss this mostly in terms of the kind of test likely to be given over the material studied, whereas we have tried to suggest that test taking is only one among many possible purposes for reading and studying.

Kind of material being studied, the second of Anderson and Armbruster's variables, has been discussed here and in Chapters 2, 6, and 7 as part of the need to make students aware of their text's organization. Within this chapter, choice of one of the three levels of study reading depends, in part, on knowledge of text structure and, of course, purpose for reading.

The student's relevant background knowledge, part of Anderson and Armbruster's third variable, has been discussed within this chapter as one of the elements of a successful study approach and is explored more fully in Chapter 1 and in Chapters 6 and 7.

The chief focus of this chapter, strategies students use in studying, is the fourth of Anderson and Armbruster's variables. Systematic study approaches, choice of text sampling technique, levels of study reading, underlining, outlining, and note taking can all be successfully used by students, according to Anderson and Armbruster, "if students process the right information in the right way" (pages 664–665).

Just as we have tried to demonstrate with the tongue-in-cheek study system called PIRACY, it does not make a great deal of difference what the various elements or variables affecting study are called—it just makes a difference that they are called something and included in our understanding of what makes for successful studying.

REFERENCES

ANDERSON, THOMAS H., AND ARMBRUSTER, BONNIE B. "Studying." In P. David Pearson, Rebecca Barr, Michael L. Kamil, and Peter Mosenthal (Eds.), *Handbook of Reading Research*. New York: Longman, 1984, pp. 657–680.

APPLEBEE, ARTHUR N. *Writing in the Secondary School: English and the Content Areas.* Urbana, IL: National Council of Teachers of English, 1981.

JOHNS, JERRY L., AND MCNAMARA, LAWRENCE P. "The SQ3R Study Technique: A Forgotten Research Target," *Journal of Reading, 23,* 1980, 705–708.

MCCONKIE, GEORGE W., AND RAYNER, KEITH. "The Span of the Effective Stimulus During a Fixation in Reading," *Perception and Psychophysics, 17,* 1975, 578–586.

PEARSON, P. DAVID, AND TIERNEY, ROBERT J. "Toward a Composing Model of Reading," *Language Arts, 60,* 1984, 568–580.

ROBINSON, H. ALAN. *Effective Study.* New York: Harper and Row, 1961.

VACCA, RICHARD T., AND VACCA, JO ANNE L. *Content Area Reading,* 2nd ed. Boston: Little, Brown, 1986.

WITTY, PAUL A. "Rate of Reading: A Crucial Issue," *Journal of Reading, 13,* 1969, 102–106, 154–162.

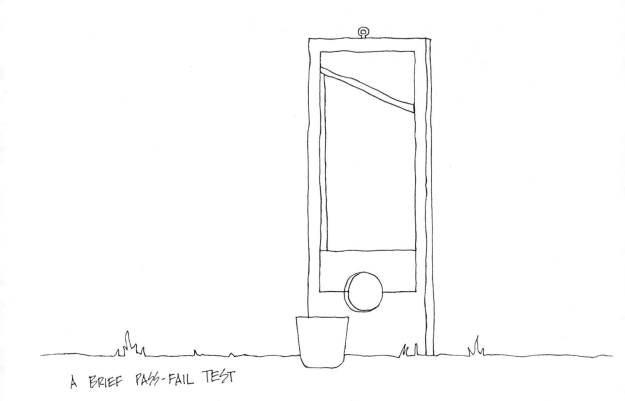

A BRIEF PASS-FAIL TEST

11

EVALUATION

Reading and writing are two tools for learning your content area. Therefore, you need some ways to evaluate, both formally and informally, how well students are reading and writing as it relates to learning your content area.

Evaluation is communication between students and yourself about their learning and your teaching. Evaluation has a much larger meaning than giving grades. You give grades for how well your students do in your content area, and we are confident you don't need this book to tell you how to grade your eleventh-grade physics class. In this chapter, evaluation refers to ways of getting information about how your students learn from their reading.

Formal reading tests exist to tell you your students' reading test scores, just as IQ tests exist to tell you your students' presumed intelligence level. Because of the implications of the overview of reading that we presented in Chapter 1, formal measures of reading, usually done on students via standardized, computer-scored tests, seem only a distant way to begin understanding your students' reading levels. After you find that Johnny and Joanie are "low readers," how do you know where the problem lies? What are your responsibilities when the problem appears to lie in the area of reading?

Formal standardized tests assess your students, but you need to

make sense of that assessment, and that sense making is called evaluation (Sax, 1980). Essentially, it involves collecting *and* making sense of data. In this chapter we advocate both processes and suggest ways to collect the information and to make sense of it.

INFORMAL EVALUATION

After Vacca and Vacca (1986), we find it convenient to group evaluation methods under *formal* and *informal*. The formal methods are those represented by standardized tests, which match your students' reading level against those of other students, perhaps nationally, or against preset criteria. These formal methods, although of value to others, seem of little use to the content area teacher, and we do not discuss them here. Far more useful are the informal methods, which allow you to see how well your students are using the learning tools of reading (and writing) in your class.

Informal means just that—no rigid guidelines exist to implement a set of procedures of informal evaluation methods. We cannot give you a step-by-step approach; instead, we suggest that you keep in mind why you need to evaluate your students' reading ability—it is one way of monitoring their learning in your class, of finding out their strengths, of locating their weaknesses, and of improving their learning and your instruction. Like reading and writing, evaluation is a process, intended to make the product (learning) better.

Evaluation helps you know if the students are doing their job. But evaluation goes two ways. It also tells you how well you are doing yours.

Why Evaluate Informally?

In an interesting study (Nicholson, 1984), a group of researchers observed every classroom reading activity in two classes of thirteen- and fourteen-year olds during six months. The content areas included social studies, mathematics, English, and science. The definition of reading was quite broad, involving anything to do with print, such as formulas and diagrams as well as text. They found that although the students appeared to be learning, they were actually in "a maze of confusion" (p. 436).

For example, when two junior high students were asked how they had arrived at creating a perfect bar graph in social studies, the observers instantly realized that the students did not understand at all what they had graphed. The students did not understand the words *urban* and *rural*, even though they had graphed the urban and rural population of New Zealand. The product—the bar graph—did not reveal the students' confusion, and the students had not learned the concepts' relation to population.

Similarly, students did not realize that a definition of a new word, *photosynthesis*, existed in the text they were reading. One student interpreted *diameter* as the dot in the middle of a circle on a diagram. Another could not understand a diagram explaining water cycles. Frequently, students could not pick out the key ideas in a passage.

These were not unusual or particularly weak students; they were skilled hiders of confusion about issues the teacher thought they knew. When we give an algebra test, we know if students get the right or wrong answers. Informal evaluation, however, can clue us in to the reason that a student could not solve "$2x = 8$" is because he or she is used to interpreting x as multiplication. In the Nicholson study, it was exactly such little things that confused students, but without informal methods of evaluation, the teacher did not find out—and therefore could not correct—the problems.

In mathematics, physics, and many other subjects, students' background knowledge can lead to misconceptions that make teaching a difficult job. Interpreting x as multiplication can throw off an algebra lesson, just as interpreting *market* as the supermarket will lead to misunderstandings during a lecture on global economics.

The confusions uncovered by the Nicholson study were caused by many sources. One of the reasons related to the students' background knowledge, which is one of the variables in our definition of reading. Another related to lack of vocabulary knowledge, or semantics, which is another of the variables in our definition of reading. The implication is that with any of the variables, including attention, attitude, and purpose, the reading or comprehension process might break down, making it harder for you to achieve your teaching goals.

Because we know students can get the right answer for the wrong reasons, as with the bar graph of urban and rural populations, we need ways of communication between ourselves and students. Discussion and small-group work are important ways, allowing you access to the understanding of students.

Another important way is the journal that we discussed at length in Chapter 8. One of the main benefits of journal writing is as an informal evaluation tool for teachers, to see how and what and why students are learning. Reading a student's journal can help you find out where a student needs help *before* he or she fails an exam. Moreover, reading a journal can help you find out where a student needs help even though the student may have correctly completed an assignment. It reveals students' misconceptions and confusions.

EVALUATION BASED ON A DEFINITION OF READING

We propose using the definition of reading outlined in Chapter 1 as a simple framework for locating where reading problems lie. As we mentioned in Chapter 1, the physiological and phonological components are out of the scope of this book, and syntax is in place for most students. We are most interested in evaluating the elements relating to semantics, experience, attitude, purpose, and motivation. In the following section we suggest at least one way to gather information on each element and what to do with the information once collected. If you find that your students have a problem with one of these elements, you have a direction for adapting your teaching.

Evaluation, for our purposes, means gathering some information *and* making sense out of it. It is, of course, a two-part process. The first is deciding what information to gather. We will describe some kinds of information we have found valuable and describe some ways to record that information. The second part, the making sense part, is the most important and most difficult. We will give some examples and lead you through the interpretation process.

Semantics

In assessing the semantic component of a student's reading ability, you need a sense of the student's ability to use the words in reading and easily make sense of reading material. If you are interested in collecting information about that ability, or semantics, a good method is the *cloze* procedure. In Chapter 3 we discussed readability formulas as one way to predict whether a given book is appropriate for a given grade level; now we suggest a way to see whether a student's general reading ability is appropriate for a given book. Even if we have a text with, presumably, an appropriate reading level for a class, the students in it will have reading levels that vary above and below grade level. It would be helpful for you to determine how well the match is between the textbook you will use and your students' ability to understand it. If you find that most students can understand the textbook itself, you can be more confident that the book is adequate for helping you to teach the concepts. But if students cannot read the book, it will not help you teach.

In the cloze procedure, words are deleted from a passage. A useful way to develop evaluation is to locate three passages from your textbook, from the first one-third, second one-third, and third one-third of the book. Leave the first sentences (or paragraphs) from the passages as is, so that students can use them for context. Delete every fifth word from the middle section, replacing them with spaces of equal length. Have the students fill in the blanks before they have read the passage in the book.

You can try taking a cloze test yourself with the following three paragraphs from later in this chapter:

A good way to get a sense of what a student brings to the material is by use of a pretest. We talked about prediction and other prereading techniques in Chapters 6 and 7 as ways of bringing out and developing a student's knowledge of content before reading. The journal, as we discussed in Chapter 8, is another way. In this chapter we _____ interested in how to _____ out what students already _____. We have been guilty _____ assuming that a class _____ knows about something because _____ student makes a knowledgeable _____ or because several students _____ their heads. The danger _____ in assuming existing or _____ knowledge and passing over _____ content too quickly.

A _____ is a good way _____ pick up on students' _____, to show you and _____ what they already know, _____ to indicate directions a _____ or unit needs to _____ on. If you discuss _____ results immediately, you can _____ up misconceptions and foreshadow _____ main events in an _____ unit. Drawing from their _____ is a strength, but _____ also need some kind _____ summary statement from you. _____ written pretests give you _____ sense of where your _____ strengths and weaknesses are, _____ you do not grade _____ but simply scan them _____ get a sense of _____ students already know or _____ they have misconceptions.

For _____, it is well known _____ students have difficulties with _____ such as the laws _____ motion because the laws _____ follow what the students _____ been observing all of _____ lives. Similarly, students have _____ with symbols such as _____, because they read them _____ arrows signifying only direction. _____ often have common beliefs _____, say, a particular war _____ only one cause.

Students' responses will show you if they can read the passage and how well they understand it. To get the score, read the passage to them and let them mark the correct guesses. (You will find the example under the heading Experience on page 162.) Count as correct *only exact replacements.* You're buying yourself trouble by allowing synonyms, and it is not worth your time trying to allow for the choice of *very* when the word was *quite.* The formula is generous and allows for this.

Calculate the percentage correct by dividing the number right by the total number of blanks. Use the following scale to interpret the findings. If you have a well-constructed multiple-choice test, it should compare with the following percentages for cloze:

Percent Correct

Cloze	*Multiple-Choice Test*
57% or more	100%
50%	90%
38%	75%
	(Bormuth, 1958)

Spread the cloze tests out over a few days during the first week of class. A word of caution: Students are not used to accepting that 50 percent correct is considered a very good job, thus this procedure can be frustrating for them. Explain to them exactly what you are doing and why.

In order to show a class of student teachers for themselves what the experience of cloze is, we gave them two passages, one from a piece of nonfiction (a biography written in fictional style) and one from a book on learning a computer language. We found that the cloze technique rather accurately divorced students' knowledge of content from their ability to read. Remember, with cloze you do not want to measure your students' knowledge of your content area but rather their general reading ability, to see whether your text is a good enough match for them. We found that the background of students did not influence their performance on the two passages. Students who were nonprogrammers did as well on the programming passages as students who teach mathematics and computer science. In fact, some of the English teachers did better with the computer passage than with the fictional style, even though they are nonprogrammers. The biography with its fictional techniques appeared to have more possibilities for word choice.

Cloze tests are quite useful. Cloze gives you good information about students' ability to read the text. It is *one* way of matching the fit between text and students. You can identify serious problems and find alternative methods of getting information to those students.

If many students in your class have difficulties with making sense of words in your text, as revealed by cloze, look carefully at how vocabulary is introduced in the text. If the text does not do a good job, you may have to compensate. Perhaps some work with context clues, as outlined in Chapter 4, is a partial solution. Perhaps the students need more work with following text aids, as discussed in Chapter 2. Or perhaps the text is so difficult for the particular group of students that you need to supplement it with other sources of information. You are not a reading teacher. If your goal is to teach your content area, you need to figure out other ways to get information to a student who cannot understand a textbook. A good reader can read into a recorder, and a weak reader can follow along with the text. A weak reader can find information from other sources such as filmstrips, movies, video, computers, and so on. The media resources person at your school can help you explore these options. Your goal is not to turn the student into a reader of your content area but to give the student information that you have deemed important about it, why the discipline is important, and how it relates to the way we live and to the student's own life.

If many students have trouble with the text, the problem lies with the book. If they do well on the cloze test, you have a good opportunity to praise them about what they already know.

Syntax

Strictly speaking, your students' ability to make sense of word order, or syntax, should be in place by secondary school. Although we consider syntax out of the scope of this book, a high readability score or poor performance on the cloze test may indicate that the sentences are too convoluted and unclear. If your students replace adjectives with verbs, for example, they haven't the vaguest idea of what is going on and may be unable to profit from the text. Poetry, of course, is a special case, requiring a different reading of syntax.

Experience

A good way to get a sense of what a student brings to the material is by use of a pretest. We talked about prediction and other prereading techniques in Chapters 6 and 7 as ways of bringing out and developing a student's knowledge of content before reading. The journal, as we discussed in Chapter 8, is another way. In this chapter we are interested in how to find out what students already know. We have been guilty of assuming that a class already knows about something because one student makes a knowledgeable comment or because several students nod their heads. The danger lies in assuming existing or correct knowledge and passing over important content too quickly.

A pretest is a good way to pick up on students' misconceptions, to show you and them what they already know, and to indicate directions a lesson or unit needs to concentrate on. If you discuss the results immediately, you can clear up misconceptions and foreshadow the main events in an upcoming unit. Drawing from their experience is a strength, but students also need some kind of summary statement from you. The written pretests give you a sense of where your students' strengths and weaknesses are, as you do not grade them but simply scan them to get a sense of what students already know or where they have misconceptions.

For example, it is well known that students have difficulties with concepts such as the laws of motion because the laws don't follow what the students have been observing all of their lives. Similarly, students have trouble with symbols such as vectors, because they read them as arrows

signifying only direction. Students often have common beliefs that, say, a particular war had only one cause.

A pretest can have many forms. If you want to test for simple facts, then you can ask short-answer, fill-in-the-blank, or even simple true-or-false questions. Follow up the test immediately, focusing not only on whether a question is true or false but also *why* the answer is as it is. This is, of course, also bridge building.

If you wish to test for knowledge *and* relationship or sequence of ideas, you might wish to draw up a partially blank outline or map of some kind. For example, we show here a partial outline to use as a pretest on the Civil War, to see the extent of students' knowledge. You will learn if they can give one or two major differences in each section.

Pretest on Civil War

Origins of the Civil War
  I. Economic differences between the North and South
     A.
     B.
     C.
 II. Cultural differences between the North and South
     A.
     B.
     C.

III. Population differences between the North and South
    A.
    B.
    C.

You will notice that a pretest works as a prereading technique. Your students encounter ideas in the pretest, drawing on their background experience, and adding to their knowledge during the follow-up discussion. They have more to bring to the reading. In the Civil War example, the differences in economics, culture, and population would be a main focus of the discussion, and you want to see what students already know about it.

How does a teacher construct a "good" pretest? The pretest should relate to teacher purpose, selected from main ideas and objectives you wish to teach or that you think students misunderstand. Such a pretest gives students an expectation or direction about what the unit will be on. Another aspect of a good pretest is that students will display whatever it is they do know. If all answers are blank, you have no information, and the pretest is too frustrating for the student. Construct the pretest so that students can answer some of the questions. And, essential to successful use of pretests, is discussion right after students take them.

You have probably thought of other excellent methods for assessing the background experience that students bring to a new unit—in their journals, in discussion, in small-group work, and so on.

Attitude/Purpose/Motivation

In Chapter 1 we stated that attitude, purpose, and motivation can help or hinder learning, particularly from reading. In this chapter we suggest some ways to gather information about these three elements.

Attitude about your content area or the textbook can be positive, and if so you have no problems in this area. Frequently, however, students either dislike or are afraid of a subject. For example, many students fear mathematics, "hard" sciences, writing, or poetry. If you find that a major hindrance to a student's learning is fear of your subject, you can help by creating an environment for success and clearing up confusion. If you can see attitude improving during the course of a unit or a year, you can feel better about your own approach to teaching. Thus, it might be worthwhile to chart over time some measure about a student's attitude, as we suggest below.

Purpose, as we have stated, is the teacher's responsibility. As teachers, we have strong purposes for what we teach and for why students should read a particular passage, for example. But frequently students do not understand the purpose of what they are doing. If informal evaluation reveals that your students do not understand why they are doing what they do in your class, you can remedy the problem by making objectives clearer to them. You can rethink and redirect your purpose if students suddenly appear not to understand why they have to do something. Students shouldn't have to wonder what the purpose is; find out if they understand it.

Motivation, as all teachers know, can be difficult to influence. We think that where the student has been well informed about the purpose for the work done, and where the student's attitude, experience, and general reading ability have been considered, the motivation should be influenced positively. Therefore, if you sense that your class is lacking in motivation, you would do well to assess the other elements of our definition of reading in Chapter 1. A student's claim that a class is "boring" can be a student's defense for not understanding the class or the text, for example.

If you believe motivational problems do not stem from any deficiency with the other elements, you might want to gather information about what motivates students, such as praise, learning, grades, peer approval, and so on. Find out what students expect or want. You can emphasize group work, for example, if students seem more motivated by peer approval.

Informal data collection methods are not the only possibilities for gathering information about attitude, purpose, and motivation. Obvious methods are journals, as discussed in Chapter 8, or class discussion. If you want to gain information about attitude, purpose, and motivation, other good ways are from notes and observational checklists.

Notes are informal observations you make about students related to a particular potential problem area. These need to be as simple to record as possible and quick to record and review. Teachers do not have time for massive record keeping, and the longer and more complicated records become the less likely they are to be used. If you want to record something about students' attitude, apparent motivation, and/or understanding of purpose, then notes give you a useful structure to record quickly and to review quickly. A chart is most useful if looking for change, as in Table 11–1. You could keep a record for a few students who appear to have a problem, or for a particular class that you teach.

Such a chart with notes helps you see changes over time. If a few students reveal a negative attitude, you can speak to them about it, ap-

Table 11.1   Example of a Chart for Recording Notes About Attitude, Purpose, and Motivation Three Times During the Year

	Attitude	Purpose	Motivation
Student name: _____			
September	Fears math	Thinks answering questions is goal	Grades only
December			
March			

peal to them more frequently than before, or praise them when they succeed.

Observational checklists resemble notes except that you might further divide comments into categories, such as numbers from 1 to 5 for low attitude to high attitude. A numbered chart is quick and easy to record and read, particularly when you wish to see change over time.

Notes and observational checklists are worth the time and trouble only if you are feeling uneasy that the problems of some students lie in a particular area.

CLOSING STATEMENT

Informal evaluation is a way of making judgments about the class and your success as a teacher. With these methods, you can get a sense of the class in advance and after instruction. We do not suggest that you routinely run down every element of the definition of reading to assess your students' ability to profit from the text. Rather, we suggest that you use it to find out where a problem might lie so that you can take steps to improve students' general abilities to use textbooks to learn about your content area. If a student has strength in a particular element, move on to something else.

The only reason to do evaluation is for purposes of planning for improved instruction, the topic of the next chapter. Planning causes the use of evaluation. We plan for a teaching objective and modify those plans based on what we know about students from our methods of evaluation.

REFERENCES

BORMUTH, JOHN R. "The Cloze Readability Procedure." In John R. Bormuth (Ed.), *Readability in 1968*. Urbana, IL: National Council of Teachers of English, 1968.

NICHOLSON, TOM. "Experts and Novices: A Study of Reading in the High School Classroom," *Reading Research Quarterly, 19*, 1984, 436–451.

SAX, GILBERT. *Principles of Educational and Psychological Measurement and Evaluation*, 2nd ed. Belmont, CA: Wadsworth, 1980.

VACCA, RICHARD T., AND VACCA, JO ANNE L. *Content Area Reading*, 2nd ed. Boston: Little, Brown, 1986.

12

PLANNING

In this chapter we regroup ideas from previous chapters into a discussion of a three-part lesson plan. We argue that all reading lesson plans should include prereading, reading, and postreading components, becoming a three-part lesson plan as shown here. Far from making your planning rigid, this three-part scheme allows great flexibility and variety, while at the same time enabling your students to learn the most about your content area from the text.

A Three-Part Lesson

Planning for Content Area Reading

PREREADING
  A. Purpose setting
  B. Bridge building
  C. Vocabulary instruction
READING
  A. Study skills *
  B. Readability level **
  C. Text structure *

*Application of skills previously taught.
**Measured before text is used.

POSTREADING
   A. Discussion, application, or writing activity keyed to reading purpose, and/or vocabulary review
   B. Evaluation
   C. Review/preview

THREE-PART LESSON PLAN

Prereading

Prereading instruction involves purpose setting, leading to a multitude of possibilities for prereading activities, including bridge building and vocabulary instruction.

Purpose Setting.   Purpose setting has three major parts—deciding what is to be learned, modifying the objectives based on the students and what they know, and making clear where the lesson fits.

Deciding what students should learn is the first part of purpose setting. Part of the decision making for determining the objectives for the lesson can be thought out even before you meet the students. Choosing these learning objectives involves, in part, decisions about three levels of understanding. Should the learning be literal? If so, you will focus on facts to be mastered. Should it be inferential? In that case, you want students to think about facts, make connections, or structure knowledge. Should the learning be higher-than-inferential? If so, you need ways of getting at affect (attitude, and such), and also appreciation and experience. Higher-than-inferential also includes placing the discipline in perspective ("Why is biology important?" "How does mathematics relate to me?" "How does one do history?"). As we suggested in Chapter 6, selecting questions on three levels in light of your purpose is one excellent way of arriving at your objectives.

The second part, modifying the objectives based on the students' abilities and needs, involves incorporating the information you know about your students and evaluating their learning, their ability to profit from the text, and your success in teaching. In Chapter 11 we discussed some ways to modify your purpose setting based on evaluation. When you wish to find out what your students already know about a new unit, you need to assess their experience. A pretest followed by discussion might get at that information. Keying questions to all levels might also help as a pretest or preunit discussion. Prediction strategies, as discussed in Chapters 6 and 7, also can indicate how much your students already know and understand about a topic.

The third part, making clear where the lesson fits, involves making a connection between past and future units and between the known and the unknown. If you make clear how a new topic fits with what went before, with what students know, and with how the topic relates to what follows, students will understand the purpose better. For example, if you are beginning a unit on poetry, you might start with this list: affect, language, sound, appreciation, why people need to express themselves in poetry, and the nature of poetry. One of the hardest questions students ask is, "Why should I study this?" As part of purpose setting before reading, you need to think about this difficult question.

Instruction Based on Purpose Setting. In this book we refer to many techniques for reading instruction, such as discussion, small-group work, questioning, and so on. None of these can be pigeon-holed into only a prereading, reading, or postreading technique. It can be appropriate to teach vocabulary, for example, during any part of the lesson. Deciding when to use a technique varies according to your purpose.

When your evaluation tells you that a reading passage contains much unknown material for students, your role, as we have said before, is to "build the bridge" between the known and the unknown (Pearson and Johnson, 1978). This bridge building makes the reading and therefore the learning easier. You might want to preview the reading for the students, to ask questions eliciting what they know, to design an activity in which they encounter concepts similar to those in the reading (an experiment in science, for example). Vocabulary instruction as a prereading activity often involves words unknown by the students—words that are crucial to the understanding of a passage. By spending time with such terminology before reading, you heighten the chances that your students will recognize the words and understand their reading better. Among the constellation of techniques discussed in this book is prediction. Prediction gives a sense of where a passage is going, a sense that a student can test when reading.

Reading

In discussing reading, we leave it up to you to decide whether students should read in class or out and how many pages they should read. These decisions are determined by your purpose and your evaluation of

students. Rather, we are interested in the many ways you can help students gain more from their reading.

Determining the difficulty of the text is one aspect of this. You might examine the readability score (Chapter 3) in conjunction with students' scores on a cloze test (Chapter 11) to evaluate how well their general reading ability matches the text.

You can also assist students enormously by spending a small amount of class time introducing the text (Chapter 2) and teaching the use of text aids such as headings, boldface type, index, glossary, and so on. Making sure that students understand the importance of varying their rate of reading and skimming and scanning or rereading (Chapter 10) helps students who plod along word-for-word. Also, heightening students' awareness of the value of monitoring their comprehension makes them more independent about their own reading. You cannot constantly be telling students to take particular note of boldface headings, to reread when they don't understand, or to use the glossary, but an excellent way of working with these ideas is to spend a few class periods near the beginning of the year with direct instruction and then occasionally to model your own thinking processes aloud as you read to them.

Students benefit considerably from a little instruction in recognizing context clues and using structural analysis (Chapter 4), so that they can interpret the meaning of new words by using the context and parts of words, thus becoming less dependent on you for direct instruction.

With difficult passages, you can guide the reading by creating worksheets with questions to answer while reading. Questions at different levels encourage different levels of thinking. You can also encourage students to take notes or use other study strategies discussed in Chapter 10.

Finally, you can ease the reading of a text by making sure that students understand the basis on which they will be evaluated. Your purpose guides their reading.

Postreading

In activities after reading, your interest is in what was learned, how the reading added to what was known, and how the reading fit in with what went before.

Obvious candidates are quizzes and tests, with questions from three levels. Discussion is perhaps the most frequent, again based on the three levels of questions. Vocabulary understanding can be deepened after reading, particularly when your goal is production of vocabulary. For example, students can do a word sort in small groups (Chapter 5) to chart the relationships of important concepts. Mapping, clustering, and other study techniques (Chapter 11) help deepen the students' understanding and retention of the reading material. Journals (Chapter 8) provide a forum for reflecting on the reading, and more public writing (Chapter 9) allows students to communicate about what they learned.

What you do in the postreading phase can foreshadow your next unit and can help you with purpose setting next time.

OTHER WAYS OF LOOKING AT PLANNING

Anderson and Armbruster (1984), citing Cunningham et al., list what might be called the desiderata of successful reading comprehension lessons. There appear to be five components common to successful comprehension lessons. They are:

1. Readiness. This is what we have referred to as bridge building, and it involves bringing out what students already know about the topic and adding to that, as necessary, the background the author has assumed was in place.

2. Purpose setting.

3. Students read for the purpose stated.

4. Performance. The students do something that reflects whether they have succeeded at the reading. (This might be a discussion, quiz, or some other product.)

5. Feedback. Basically, let the students know as specifically and as quickly as possible how they did.

You will note that all of these elements are included in a three-part lesson plan.

CLOSING STATEMENT

The three-part reading lesson plan discussed here is a cycle. Each lesson builds on the one before and prepares for the next. Thus, planning occurs before, during, and after reading.

The before part, purpose setting, bridge building, and vocabulary instruction, are all informed by your understanding of your students on a host of dimensions. And that understanding is informed by your students' reactions to previous lessons.

The during part, use of study skills, prediction of reading difficulty, and use of text structure and text aids, tells you whether your prereading

instruction was successful and gives you some direction for your postreading activities.

The after part, discussion, activity, evaluation, and preview/review, close out the current lesson and set the stage for the next lesson or lessons.

And so it goes. As we implied at the beginning, this chapter does not present any new information. It is simply the whole book looked at through a long lens.

REFERENCES

ANDERSON, THOMAS H., AND ARMBRUSTER, BONNIE B. "Studying." In P. David Pearson, Rebecca Barr, Michael L. Kamil, and Peter Mosenthal (Eds.), *Handbook of Reading Research*. New York: Longman, 1984, pp. 657–680.

PEARSON, P. DAVID, AND JOHNSON, DALE. *Teaching Reading Comprehension*. New York: Holt, Rinehart and Winston, 1978.

INDEX

AUTHORS

SUBJECTS